The Native Game

The Native Game

Settler Perceptions of Indian/Settler Relations in Central Labrador

Evelyn Plaice

Social and Economic Studies No. 40
Institute of Social and Economic Research
Memorial University of Newfoundland

© Institute of Social and Economic Research 1990
Memorial University of Newfoundland
St. John's, Newfoundland
Canada
ISBN 0-919666-63-9

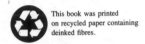

Canadian Cataloguing in Publication Data
Plaice, Evelyn Mary, 1955-

The native game

(Social and economic studies, ISSN 0847-0898 ; no. 40)
Based on the author's thesis (M.A.)--Memorial University
of Newfoundland, 1987.
Includes bibliographical references.
ISBN 0-919666-63-9

1. North West River (Nfld.) -- Social conditions -- History.
2. North West River (Nfld.) -- Ethnic relations -- History.
3. Ethnicity -- Newfoundland -- North West River.
4. Group identity -- Newfoundland -- North West River.
5. Indians of North America -- Newfoundland -- North West River.
I. Memorial University of Newfoundland. Institute of Social
and Economic Research. II. Title. III. Series: Social and economic
studies (St. John's, Nfld.) ; no. 40.

HN110.N67P52 1990   305'.8'0097182   C90-097600-4

In memory of
Michael John Buck
January 22nd 1945–September 6th 1988

North West River looking east from Upalong towards the centre of town and Baikie's Point, with the south bank on the right. Circa 1940.
Credit: Courtesy of Bella Shouse and *Them Days* Photo Archive.

Contents

Acknowledgements   ix
Preface   xi
1   Introduction   1
2   The History of European Settlement and   11
    Development in the Hamilton Inlet Region
3   Geographical Orientation to the Community   43
4   Kith and Kin   52
5   Them Days   63
6   Bridge Apart   74
7   Upalong-Downalong   88
8   Leemos!   101
9   Conclusion   120
Notes   124
References   134
ISER Books   142

Maps and Photographs

Map 1: Labrador   xii
Map 2: Dispersed Settlement in the Lake Melville Region   44
Map 3: Residential Areas in North West River   47
Photo Portfolio One: 1875–1958   Follows page 42
Photo Portfolio Two: 1930–1979   Follows page 100

Acknowledgements

The warmth and friendship I encountered in North West River during the winter of 1983–84 (and on many previous visits) resulted in the critical journey through the heart of one small northern Canadian community which is presented in this book. The book belongs in spirit to the members of that community. This interpretation of community life is a personal one, and I apologize here for any misunderstanding which may arise.

For any coherent piece of work to emerge from the chaos of fieldwork and endless writing requires the encouragement and interest of many people. I would like to acknowledge the following people for their critical discussion, guidance, enthusiasm, and logistic and moral support: Fred Aldrich, Peter Armitage, Aunt Edna Campbell and family, Kat Cooper and family, Sarah Cully and family (especially Jess), Frummie Diamond, Anne Douglas, Jeanette Gleeson, Gordon Inglis, John Kennedy, Marguerite MacKenzie, Jim MacLean, Susan Nichol, Judy Norman, Julie O'Hollaren, Robert Paine, George and Alice Park, Helen Peters, John, Eileen and David Plaice, Joanne Prindiville, Nigel Rapport, Phil Ross, Jeremy Shapiro, Rowena Simson and family, John Steckley, Adrian Tanner, Janice Udell, Kurt Wolfe and many others—thank you. Although now incorporated into work for which I take the responsibility, their contributions frequently had a profound influence on the shaping of this book.

Two people above all others gave their unstinting support in this endeavour: Jean Briggs and Ron Schwartz. Jean spent hours helping me unravel the skeins of complex data which resulted from fieldwork and writing, forcing me always to be clear and insightful. Ron gave me the faith, courage and companionship I needed in order to write. They have my admiration, love and thanks.

The research for this book was supported by monies from Memorial University of Newfoundland and the Institute of Social and Economic Research. The staff of ISER books, especially Robert Paine, have been heroes in the crusade to get this manuscript into book form. It has been launched with much more than just their blessing. I sincerely hope it proves to be a project worthy of their loyalty!

Evie Plaice
Manchester   March 1990

Preface

So pretty it looks in the fall when we come home from our summer quarters, above 70 miles from here. When we are sailing up in our large boat, to see the ducks in our bay when we are nearing the river, and when we get ashore to the pretty river banks and walking up the path under our large trees, some 50 feet and some 60 feet high, we often meet with a flock of partridges flying up to the trees. Before we get to the house, so pretty, then is the scramble among the young ones who will see the first turnips and potatoes, and sure enough all around the house is green with turnip tops, and between them and the wall of the house is hanging red with moss berries, some falls. Then we get home to our winter house for ten months more (Campbell 1980:2–3).[1]

The description is of Mulligan, a small seasonal settlement. It is not far from the community of North West River, which lies at the head of Hamilton Inlet, the deep fjord which bisects the Labrador land mass. As is true of all deep fjords, the head of Hamilton Inlet is rich in wildlife and vegetation because it is sheltered some 170 miles inland from the North Atlantic, yet it still forms part of Labrador's 11,000 miles of coastline. The four permanent communities—Happy Valley-Goose Bay, Mud Lake, Sheshatshit and North West River—situated at the head of the Inlet are home to approximately 9,000 Indians, Inuit, Settlers, and 'come-from-aways.' North West River has a population of 500 Settlers; the neighbouring Indian community of Sheshatshit, until 1979 part of North West River, has a population of approximately 500 Innu.

Labrador is the easternmost section of the Canadian or Laurentian Shield, and lies on the northeastern edge of the North American continent facing Baffin Island to the north and Greenland to the north-east. It has a triangular land mass of approximately 112,000 square miles, with a population of approximately 36,500, which

Map 1: Labrador

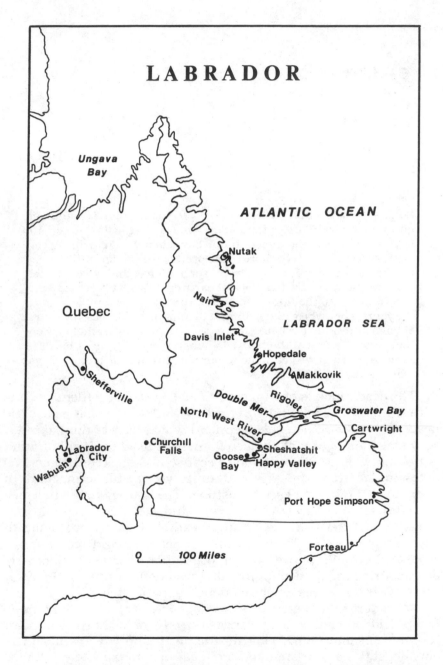

Cartography: Donald Battcock

means that most of Labrador is scarcely populated, especially since more than two-thirds of the people live in the three urban centres of Wabush-Labrador City, Churchill Falls, and Happy Valley-Goose Bay. The urban population is largely composed of 'come-from-aways,' such as mainland Canadians and Newfoundlanders, while the remaining third of the population is a mixture of Indians, Inuit and Settlers.[2] These indigenous peoples have diverse cultural and historical backgrounds, and mostly live in small, isolated communities along the coast. The communities are reached year round (weather permitting) by light aircraft (Labrador Airways), and by coastal ferry service (run by CN Marine) during the shipping season, which is between late June and October. Land-based activities are still culturally significant in Central Labrador, despite the fact that wage-labour now predominates in the economy.[3]

Spring begins as the snow leaves the land, and summer is short and intense. The weather usually becomes warm and dry towards the end of April, and in May the Settlers hunt seals on the old winter ice in Lake Melville and Hamilton Inlet. Salmon fishing starts in early June—as soon as the ice leaves the water.[4] The run is followed out to the Atlantic, ending in late July. A considerable amount of market gardening takes place at the head of the Inlet during the hot, dry weeks of mid-summer. Other summer activities include cod fishing, for which several North West River families migrate temporarily to summer quarters in Groswater Bay, and berry picking, which is carried out on their return during late summer and early fall. Separate trips are made in September and October to hunt migratory waterfowl and seabirds. In summer and while the water remains open, people travel by boat because most of the settlements and the camps from which people hunt, fish and trap are situated along the shore. The waterways serve as transportation routes in both summer and winter.

Snow may arrive as early as September, but usually comes in earnest in October, heralded by the passage of snow buntings migrating from the north. During the active years of the fur trade, trappers set out for their traplines by canoe at this time of year; at present, only limited hunting and trapping takes place inland during the fall and winter. Most North West River Settlers have the use of a cabin, situated along one of the rivers or lakes, for hunting and trapping. Ice forms over the small lakes in October, and is formed and broken by storms several times throughout November in Lake Melville and Hamilton Inlet. Once the ice forms solidly across the main stretches of water, transportation is by snowmobile, snowshoes and skis. However, there is always a tedious wait while freeze-up and break-up, the transitions from land and water to snow and ice, take place when travel of most sorts is curtailed.

I became interested in Labrador at the end of my high school career, when I spent a year as a volunteer for the International Grenfell Association before continuing with my education. The International Grenfell Association has provided the inhabitants of Labrador with various health and social services since its inception in 1892. At that time Newfoundland, with its mainland portion of Labrador, was a British colony. The Association's administration and financial backing came initially from charities in Britain, but with Confederation in 1949, the organization came under the mandate of the Canadian Government. Still, the use of volunteers from Britain, America and Canada continued until quite recently.

The experiences of my first year in Newfoundland and Labrador, in 1974–75, convinced me that I wanted to study anthropology. I returned for a further six months of voluntary work with the International Grenfell Association in 1976–77, and, following this, spent the summer of 1979 in North West River carrying out field research for an undergraduate honours dissertation (Plaice 1980). These brief visits served to give me an appreciation of the pace of change and its effects on the lives of the North West River inhabitants. I returned to carry out fieldwork for the present book between September 1983 and March 1984. Although my interest was initially with all the ethnic groups to be found in Labrador, I had become increasingly drawn to the Settler communities. And so, in 1983, it was the Settlers of North West River who formed the focus of my study.

The North West River Settler population has experienced complex and radical changes in its economic, political and social fabric. People were, and still are, attracted to the community for a variety of reasons. Indian, Inuit, French, English, Scottish, and Newfoundland ancestries are represented in different families. Some of the original Settlers came as pioneers, some came later as trappers and others later still as administrators and professional workers in various service industries (such as teaching and nursing). Family identity is important within the community, and, despite the many different reasons for being in North West River, affiliation to the community is strong.

Through my field research, then, I intend to examine two fundamental aspects of Indian/Settler relations. I shall explore not only how the community's past and present problems affect Indian/Settler relations, but also what part individual family histories have played in the formation of contemporary Settler perceptions of these relations.

My original hypothesis was that Settlers were not unanimous in their perceptions of Indian/Settler relations. I felt that the various perceptions that Settlers held of Indians and Indian/Settler relations were the result of the diverse historical experiences of the community, and these could be traced by examining individual and family histories in the community.

The experience of arriving in the community in order to do 'fieldwork' daunted me. On my first trips to the community my purpose had been employment with the International Grenfell Association, and the unstructured nature of anthropological research was in contrast to my earlier experiences of working set hours at the hospital or children's homes. I could not, at first, begin to conceive of how I was to achieve the collection of data that I needed for my research during this visit, and yet I had to construct an itinerary. In order to do this, I had to examine the meaning of being an anthropologist studying a community. My opportunity came through my own oversight.

After I had been in the community for a few days, the mayor of the town asked to see me. She wanted to know whether I had obtained the consent of the town council and the community in order to proceed with my study. In my embarrassment at not having arranged to see her sooner, I offered to write about my project in the town council's newsletter, which was distributed to all members of the community. This I did,[5] and was quite astonished to hear about myself during a televised news bulletin the following week. Soon after this, a reporter from the local radio network arrived to interview me about my fieldwork. I was no longer reticent about studying the community after these encounters, nor were the community members hesitant about my presence in their community—I was *their* anthropologist and a local celebrity! People were not particularly concerned about the exact nature of my research; they understood mainly that I was collecting stories of Indians. They had noticed the presence of researchers in the neighbouring Indian community of Sheshatshit, and welcomed a researcher who was showing interest, instead, in their community.

I used the two fieldwork methods of participant observation and interviewing in order to gather information, and had intended to structure the data collection around individual life histories and extended case studies. I had wanted to become acquainted with as many people as possible at an early stage in my fieldwork. In this way I would have a large pool of informants from which to draw candidates for life history studies, and be able to complete several histories within the span of my stay. However, although I established several key informants and many more general ones, I did not collect life histories. My aim to become acquainted with as many people as possible in the early stages of my fieldwork led me to begin by collecting genealogies. Most members of the community have a keen interest in their ancestry and in the region's history. I found that, by asking about their family trees, I made the acquaintance of a large number of the residents. I needed no more of an introduction than the explanation that someone's niece or nephew, cousin or grandchild, had sent me for further information on the community's 'family tree' (most inhabitants trace their ancestry back to one or two of the few pioneer families). Interviews about ancestry soon developed into extended chats about the 'old days,' and the oldtimers who populated them.

The extended case method proved to be more useful than life histories as a strategy for shaping my data collection. The seasonal activities associated with Christmas and the New Year provided me with some suitably "apt and isolated illustrations" (Gluckman 1965:235); there were two large community gatherings, and several smaller and more private affairs. Each of them allowed for speculative gossip and the airing of opinions about changes in the community, and relations with the community of Sheshatshit. In addition, such occurrences as the construction of a bridge, the closing of the hospital, the formation of teams for winter sports, discussions about the newly-opened Lion's Club, the growth of the newly established youth group, and the progress of the men's and women's Darts Leagues offered many opportunities to become involved in community activities and to study general and pervasive phenomena in the community's social structure.

I spent six months in North West River, from the end of September until the following spring, during which time I met and made excellent friends who were happy to give me information. I did not attempt to interview people formally until I had been in the community for three months. By that time both the residents and I were familiar with each other, and I had absorbed a great deal of general information about the people and their community. This meant that, during interviews, I was able to be perceptive about the significance of statements, jokes and the more subtle ways that the people had of communicating their ideas and thoughts. The informal visits and conversations of the first three months helped me to plan the subject-matter of more formal interviews and helped make acceptable the visible brandishing of the formal interview notebook and tape recorder. I asked in advance whether I could use a tape recorder when conducting a formal interview. When permission to do so was not granted—due mostly to shyness—I conducted the interviews with a notebook and pencil.

The subject matter of each interview was as much at the discretion of the interviewee as it was shaped by my questions. Initially, I asked to be told stories about trapping and about Indians. I also asked people what they felt about the changes taking place in their community, but invariably, the content of the interview shaped itself around the things that most appealed to the interviewees.

Much of my data came from observing and participating in community activities. As is usually the case in such situations, I gained some interesting insights about North West River society by inadvertently overstepping the unwritten laws of the community. For example, on my first evening I asked what was going to be happening that night, and I was told that it was 'darts night' at the local Lion's Club. Unfortunately, when I turned up and greeted the young man who had told me this, I was dismayed to find myself the only woman in the company of serious male dart players. They courteously entertained me on that first evening, but firmly told me that, in future, Tuesday darts nights were a strictly male affair. I later joined the women's Darts League, where I was responsible for causing my team to come second when it had previously been first![6]

This division of recreational activities reflected a deeper division of social activities. For instance, I found that during my visits I would be entertained by the women in the household, but if I requested an interview, I was referred to the men. Hence, much of the data I collected informally was associated with women and their social activities, but much of the formal collection of data was provided by men.

The nature of the two kinds of information is, of course, quite different. The informally gathered information provided insight into the private lives of the women I visited, whereas the formal interview material furnished me with information that the interviewees wished to impart to me about activities in the public spheres of trapping, and other such economic concerns. Trapping culture was essentially male, and although women played a significant part in the economy, it was seldom in the public sphere of activities in which the men operated. As a result, I have often concentrated on the men's perceptions of *their* activities at the expense of the women's perceptions of theirs. Nevertheless, I was present at many public and private social affairs which involved both male and female participants, and in many of the interviews, the women added comments and counter-arguments in the background, which I was able to record.

Likewise, the activities appropriate for weekdays differed from those appropriate for the weekend. I distressed my landlady by practising newly learned handicraft skills on Sundays and spending the rest of the week visiting, when, for all of her life, the reverse was true. It just did not do to sew on Sunday, because Sunday was for visiting. Sunday has always been regarded as a day of rest, and, in Labrador, the Settlers fill these days with activities they would not otherwise have time for. I explained that, for me, visiting meant 'work,' whereas sewing was a pastime that I enjoyed. Not surprisingly, people did not understand this. I discovered that community members I visited were unable to equate my visiting with work or serious activity, and this flavoured the nature of the information which I received from them. Until they were used to my visits, they encouraged me to call when they were watching the 'soap operas,' which seemed appropriate entertainment for social visitors, and hedged my calls (or were embarrassed) when they were occupied with household chores.

North West River Settlers have a European cultural ancestry; consequently, I was already familiar with at least some aspects of the community's lifestyle. I did not, therefore, suffer from severe 'culture shock.' Instead, I began to recognize the complex nature of a culture with which I had thought I was familiar. For instance, the fact that my hosts were perturbed by my insistence upon engaging in activities which, given my age and status, were obviously inappropriate to the time of day and day of the week in which I conducted them, led me to several realizations. I was uncomfortable with the 'unwork-like' aspects of my stay in the community; visiting palled unless I got some substantial information. I also realized how fine is the line which divides 'work' from 'play,' and that, in fact, as dividers of work from play, time and place are as significant as are the activities themselves.

I became aware of the 'invisible' side of the community's family tree and the Settlers' interest in it. What seemed superficially to be an interest purely in ancestry was also an obsession with the possibility of relationships which community members consider to be incestuous, and which had become almost unavoidable in a small, isolated community. My genealogical data will never be complete because of the many sensitive and 'unknown' areas of information in the community family tree.

There have been many changes in Central Labrador since I was in North West River for my fieldwork during 1983 and 1984. The most significant of these must surely be the changes brought about by the impending decision of the Department of National Defense to establish a NATO tactical weapons training Base in Labrador, using the facilities of Goose Bay Airbase. During my stay the possibility of Goose Bay Airbase expanding in such a way was not of significance to community members. The topic seldom came up in discussions while I was present, unlike the many references which were made to prospective Indian land claims.

The Department of National Defense has not yet won its petition to have the NATO base in Labrador, but the increasing military activity and attention focused on Central Labrador has now become a major topic of concern in North West River. The shared and deepening concern, among Settlers and Indians alike, over the potential loss of a valued way of life is hampered by past differences which have politically separated these two peoples. This situation is producing some very complex social and political responses among both Settlers and Indians, but this book is not the place to explore such complexities. The social and political implications of military activity in Labrador will be dealt with in a number of studies which are at present under way in Central Labrador. The aim in the present text is to focus on the topics, albeit temporal, which were of concern to Settlers during the fall, winter and spring of 1983 and 1984.

The three main points I wish to make throughout the book are: (1) that ethnic identity is self-referential, (2) that changing social environments cause a fragmentation of social identity, and (3) that, given the fragmented nature of social identity, ethnicity becomes a resource to be manipulated in the creation and communication of social identities.

The book falls into two halves. Chapters in the first half give a detailed appraisal of the historical, economic and political development of North West River and, more generally, of the Lake Melville region. In the Preface, I have described the physical setting of North West River and outlined the fieldwork methodology used in the present study. Chapter One serves as an introduction to the community of North West River, assesses the particular ethnic situation of this community in relation to other communities in Labrador, and sets out the theoretical approach used in this book.

Chapter Two, an historical overview of the European settlement and development of Central Labrador, has three sections: the first deals with early European settlement in Central Labrador; the second explores the development and structure of the Hudson's Bay Company; and the third deals with the transition of North West River from trapping to a sedentary lifestyle, and the establishment of the International Grenfell Association as the major employer in the community after the decline of the fur trade. In the chapter, I emphasize the link between the often desperate situation the pioneers left behind them in Europe and the developing Settler society of Central Labrador. This emphasis is as much in response to the interest the Settlers themselves showed during my stay as a reflection of my own curiosity.

Chapter Three describes the pattern of settlement that developed along the shores of Lake Melville in response to a seasonal harvesting regime practised by the Settlers from early settlement days onwards, and shows how elements of this pattern can be traced in the present day spatial arrangement of the North West River community. This chapter uses as primary sources of information population census statistics, church records (including graveyards), genealogies, land grant records and town plans.

Chapters in the second half (beginning at Chapter Four) explore contemporary social interaction among North West River Settlers, and reveal, through the development of social characters, the complex array of perceptions arising from the Settlers' past experiences. Chapter Four itself uses genealogical material collected in North West River to trace the development of the 'oldtimer' social character, and places this character on a continuum with 'newcomers' and 'outsiders.' The development of the 'oldtimer' character draws heavily upon the Settlers' remembered past as pioneers in Central Labrador. As such, the information gathered in the first section of Chapter Two acts as a supplement to the discussion in Chapter Four.

Using transcripts of interviews held in the community, Chapter Five illustrates the importance of the trapping way of life to Settler identity, and, in doing so, traces the creation of the 'trapper' social character. Chapter Five, then, relies upon information presented in section two of Chapter Two.

Chapter Six develops from the previous chapter, and shows the effect of sedentarization on Settler perceptions of Indian/Settler relations by exploring the changes in perception over time and within different generations in the community.

Polarization within the occupational and social structure of North West River produces the social characters of 'Upalonger' and 'Downalonger,' which are examined in Chapter Seven. Much of the polarization within the occupational and social structure in the community occurred after sedentarization, and with the arrival and growth of the International Grenfell Association—discussed in the third part of Chapter Two.

Social characters are analysed in the context of social interaction in Chapter Eight, which is the culminating ethnographic chapter.

The concluding chapter, Chapter Nine, re-examines theoretical perspectives in the light of the ethnography.

Introduction

Until recently, North West River, Labrador, was a single municipality bisected by a river and composed of approximately 500 Settlers on the north bank and 500 Indians on the south. In 1979 the Indian side was formed into an administratively separate unit called Sheshatshit. The physical division of the settlement is paralleled by the maintenance of distinct ethnic identities. Throughout the 27 years since 1961, when government first encouraged the settlement of the Indians at North West River, the two groups have remained separate. Very little social integration or interaction has taken place, and there have been few incidents of combined activities of any kind. Each group runs its own community hall, church and school, although a few facilities such as the Hudson's Bay Company store and the International Grenfell Association (IGA) hospital, both on the north bank, are shared.

In 1743 Louis Fornel, an independent trader from Quebec, established the first trading post at the site of the present-day North West River. The establishment of Fornel's post initiated a trend in which sojourning traders and pioneers—Frenchmen from Quebec and British seamen—began appearing in the Inlet. Some of these men married Inuit and subsequently settled in the region. In 1836 the Hudson's Bay Company began operations at North West River. The fur trade grew, and North West River became the regional fur trade centre by the turn of the century.[1] Revillon Freres opened a post in 1901 on the south bank, primarily to serve the Indians, and the International Grenfell Association hospital opened on the north bank in 1916.

Incursion into the Indians' hunting territory increased as trapping by Settlers expanded, and by the 1920s Settlers' traplines had filled the valleys and spread onto the 'Height of Land' (see Map 2, p. 44). This area had never been trapped before, and had previously

been regarded as exclusively Indian hunting land. The encroach-
ment contributed to starvation among the Indians, leading to their
increased dependence upon trips to the trading posts to receive
government relief (Cooke 1979; Zimmerly 1975). At this time the
Labrador-Quebec boundary was in dispute, as was Newfoundland's
jurisdiction over the Indian bands roaming the interior. The Settler
population, which fell squarely under the jurisdiction of the Newfoundland Government, expressed anger at the free reign allowed
the Indians with regard to hunting because they were not covered
by Newfoundland wildlife regulations:

> A great deal of friction arises from the fact that our Indian visitors
> are Canadian subjects and also the boundary line between Canada
> and Newfoundland-Labrador has never been settled. Hence the
> Indians can do with impunity, right alongside the Labrador man,
> what the latter is liable to be severely fined for (Paddon 1920:109).

The height of the fur trade, which came in the 1920s, was
followed by the depression of the 1930s. Prices dropped, causing a
rapid decline in fur trading. There was no substantial new means of
obtaining a living until the arrival of Goose Bay Airbase in the early
1940s. Many Settlers were attracted to the wage labour economy,
and the military operations of Goose Bay have provided a significant
amount of employment since World War II. However, from the
beginning of the 1970s the military has been withdrawing from the
area, causing unemployment.[2] North West River continued to house
the IGA hospital and its many administrative functions and services
which were the major source of employment for the community after
the decline of trapping. The hospital, too, has since closed, and the
services of the hospital and other facilities once offered in North West
River were transferred to the military hospital premises in Goose
Bay. As a result, North West River is presently facing severely
increased unemployment.

The narrows at North West River were, for several centuries, an
Indian summer camp (Fitzhugh 1972), which grew in significance
as trading posts and other services became available. Indians were
not attracted to wage labour, even when the construction of houses
by the government started in 1961; at the same time, the Indians'
subsequent sedentarization resulted in a severe restriction of their
hunting activities. Growing political awareness among Indian
groups in Canada during the 1960s led to changes in policy concerning Indian rights; the concept of aboriginal rights was re-examined,
and land claims based on aboriginal occupancy were acknowledged
(Cardinal 1969 and 1977; Manuel and Posluns 1974). Concern with

native rights and identity became organized in this province with the founding of the Native Association of Newfoundland and Labrador (NANL) in 1973. This group subsequently split into separate organizations which represent the three different native groups in the province.[3] Our concern here is with the Naskapi-Montagnais Innu Association (NMIA) which was formed in 1975. The land claim made by this group was recognized soon after the group's formation and has been under research. In consonance with their heightened political awareness, the Indians separated from North West River and their community became known as Sheshatshit in 1979.

Ethnic relations within North West River stand in marked contrast to those in the Inuit communities on the Labrador coast to the north. The boundary between Inuit and Settler identities is to some extent ambiguous, as is shown by the decision of the Labrador Inuit Association to include Settlers in the LIA and as beneficiaries in any future land claim settlement (Brice-Bennett 1977; Kennedy 1982). However, although membership is extended to them, the particular interests of the North West River Settlers, and the land they trap, are not covered by the Nain-based LIA. Historically, all Settlers had a higher level of interaction with Inuit, with whom they shared a littoral adaptation, than with Indians. The latter remained inland for most of the year, coming out to the coast only for short periods to trade. Indian/Inuit relations have always been marked by avoidance. This makes the North West River Settlers' position an interesting one: their past affiliation with Inuit is similar to that of northern Labrador communities, but their more recent affiliation with Indians and with trapping, which has drawn them inland, has largely left them out of the LIA organization.[4] Nor are they included in the land claim negotiations of the NMIA. In fact, North West River has long since lost any native status it may once have had by virtue of the Settlers' past affiliations with either the Inuit or the Indians.[5] However, there is growing Settler interest in a newly formed Metis Association.

So far there has been one substantial study of the Settler population, carried out by Zimmerly in 1975,[6] but no study of the peculiar ethnic position of the Settlers in North West River.

Indian/white relations have seldom been approached through the eyes and minds of the non-Indian participants, as is the intent of this book. In this analysis, Indians are considered only peripherally as anything more than a 'black box'[7] or invisible process, whereas the Settlers' perceptions of Indians are used as a window through which to view the development of Settler identity. The self-reflective nature of ethnic identity stems from the fact that perceptions of ethnic identity are based upon the recognition of differences between self and other. In expressing perceptions of Indians, Settlers are exploring and communicating these differences in a social arena. It follows, then, that Settler perceptions of Indians provide important clues about the Settlers themselves. Thus, an examination of the process of boundary maintenance becomes the starting point for an exploration of internal structure.

The development of internal structure does not occur in isolation from a wider social setting, and therefore, this study also aims to examine the effects that external influences have on the shaping of the Indian/Settler boundary. An analogy suggested by paleomagnetism, a phenomenon encountered in geology, illustrates the kaleidescopic effect that such influences have on the development of internal social structure. Paleomagnetism describes the retention of magnetism in rock whose position, in relation to the magnetic pole, changes throughout its history, during which time it is also subject to subterranean pressure and heat. Components of the rock take on magnetic alignments when they are in a suitable state of flux produced by the heat and pressure. One piece of rock can therefore acquire several magnetic alignments over time, each resulting from different alignments with the magnetic pole. It is as if the rock were a piece of blotting paper taking up impressions from its surroundings before being moved and absorbing different impressions in its new position which then become superimposed over the older impressions. The same principle can be applied to the 'bricolage' (Levi-Strauss 1966) of Settler perceptions of Indians, where external alignments influence internal structures, thus forming as it were, a 'socio-magnetism.' Settlers create a collage of perceptions which are continually being adjusted in order to meet the requirements of changing social contexts.

Influences from outside the Settler community have acted very much as magnetic pulls on the perceptions of Settlers, and each change in external influence has resulted in an absorption of corresponding values which are then reflected in a variety of perceptions. Any given perception may be comprised of numerous influences, since the community is in a constant state of flux. Contemporary influences are like magnetic fields, pulling the fragments of the community into an alignment which previous alignments resist. In the community at any given time, there is a struggle between old alignments and new, with many of the old alignments themselves being equally polarized. It is within this continuous state of flux that new alignments are formed, using or rejecting old structures, and the volatile nature of change provides social actors with the possibility of a multiple number of roles.

This book, then, is concerned with the experiences of Settlers in developing an ethnic identity. The survey of literature on ethnicity given below attempts to place this study within the spectrum of ethnic studies, and makes clear the tangential position of the book with regard to other theories of ethnic interaction.

The field of ethnic studies covers many aspects of group relations and identity management, including studies concerning group members versus outsiders, political managers of group identity, and boundary maintenance between different groups. A summary of the progress of ethnic studies has been attempted a number of times (e.g. Anderson and Frideres 1981; De Vos and Romanucci-Ross 1975; Epstein 1978; Keyes 1981), and, except for some salient points, does not need to be repeated here.

As a term ethnicity has eluded definition, and yet it describes a phenomenon which, according to Van den Berghe (1973:961), is ubiquitous. Social scientists working in the growing townships of the southern African copper belt[8] initially used the term "ethnicity" as an alternative to the pejorative term "tribalism." Clyde Mitchell's perceptive analysis of the Kalela dance (1956) was one of the first studies to give credence to the emergence of a distinct set of social phenomena arising from the juxtaposition of traditional (tribal) values in a modern urban context: a set of phenomena which was later to become known as ethnicity. The term has since been applied to a wide variety of social phenomena from the tribal associations of the copper belt to the complex urban settings of European immigrants in North America, where the notion of multi-culturalism has become particularly pertinent to Canadian identity (Porter 1965; Shibutani and Kwan 1965; Honigmann 1965; Mann 1970; Ossenberg 1971). More recently, it has been applied to the encapsulated position of aboriginal minorities in various contemporary Nation-states (Barth 1969; Eidheim 1971; Stymeist 1975; Tanner 1983; Paine 1985; Dyck 1985).

The premise that ethnicity could be understood by carefully cataloguing the overt cultural traits displayed by ethnic groups, such as language and religion, became untenable with the realization that both group membership and pertinent traits could be manipulated and were apt to change over time. Furthermore the composition of each emergent ethnic group can vary infinitely, and this variety adds very little to the appreciation of ethnicity. It is the fact that such groups emerge and persist which is crucial in understanding the phenomenon of ethnicity. As a result, attention has become increasingly focused upon the social, political and economic contexts in which ethnicity becomes relevant.

Barth's (1969) suggestion that the focus of ethnic studies should be the maintenance of boundaries between groups rather than the examination of the groups themselves drew attention to the fact that ethnicity is a process of communication between different ethnic groups. The resurgence of traditional values in modern contexts is largely a result of ethnic groups having new audiences in front of which to parade their cultural attributes. Barth's insight is, perhaps, the recognition that an ethnic performance needs a receptive audience; that differences have to be recognized and acknowledged.

Such differences are recognized and acknowledged between ethnic groups in a number of ways. Anderson and Frideres (1981) argue that ethnic differences are frequently communicated through conflict. In comparing ethnicity with class, Bonacich (1972) draws attention to the fact that economic differences between groups give rise to overt and implicit antagonism. Economic difference, however, is not the only criterion upon which ethnic distinctions are built — as Teal and Bai (1981) and McCall (1983) are wont to suggest; and it is seldom the only source of conflict between ethnic groups. Schwimmer (1972) draws attention to another expression of conflict between ethnic groups. He discusses the process by which, during the sun dance ceremony, the values and beliefs of the Plains Indians are set in symbolic competition with the Western values of mainstream Canadian society. Again, Braroe (1975) describes a tacit form of the acknowledgement of differences when, using Goffman's (1959) notion of the presentation of self in everyday life, he suggests that the Indian self is denigrated in everyday interactions with whites. Lithman (1978) points to much the same kind of tension when he explains that Indians prefer to remain on reserves rather than move to towns, despite the inherent economic disadvantages, because in doing so they can minimize their contact with whites.

Stymeist (1975) extends the case of withdrawal by Indians in his study of Crow Lake. For him, the Indians form a pariah group when, through the administration of special programmes and separate management, their existence generates work for the members of other ethnic groups. "Administrative determinism" (Carstens 1971) has tended to perpetuate the discordance between ethnic groups, often enhancing such problems as stigmatization in ethnic identity (Eidheim 1971; Inglis 1970).

The relevance of context and the processes of communication, particularly conflictual ones, have become focal points in the exploration of ethnicity as a social, political and economic phenomenon. The expressions of difference between groups described above are all relevant to the situation in North West River/Sheshatshit: stigmatization is experienced; avoidance is exercised; symbolic competition occurs; the fact that most Settlers are wage-earners whereas most Indians are not, gives some credence to the existence of a split labour market along ethnic lines; and, of course, government policies affect North West River/Sheshatshit no less than any other northern Canadian town.

My concern here, however, is not with the applicability of these findings to the situation in Labrador, but with the point of departure of ethnic studies at the present time. Studies such as the ones mentioned above have generally had as their focus the interactions between different ethnic groups. My focus is the interactions between members within *one* group. I wish to go behind the scenes of inter-group communication and explore how the perceptions of ethnic differences between groups are communicated within a single group. To retreat from the boundaries between ethnic groups and focus attention on the process of communication within a single group is to neither abandon the notion of a boundary nor ignore the presence of another group; it is merely the setting aside of one level of interaction in favour of another. And it is in doing so that I diverge from previous studies in ethnicity.

Most work dealing with Indian/white relations does so from the Indian point of view.[9] Very few studies analyse the attitudes held by the white groups in their interactions with Indians.[10] Of the studies mentioned above, the one carried out by Stymeist most closely parallels the approach of my book. Stymeist attempts to explain Indian/white relations in Crow Lake with reference to external influences, and explores non-Indian attitudes towards Indians in the process. However, Stymeist's study is not self-reflective in that it does not examine how the non-Indian groups in the community perceive *themselves* in relation to Indians. Nor does he take the Indian/white relationship as a starting-point for further study, but makes the relationship the focus of the study.

This book is not solely the study of an interface between two groups; it is the study of the meaning of ethnic and other differences to members of *one* community, and of how these meanings have been shaped by external influences to produce social identities within that group. The identities which are thus constructed become ethnic identities when they are constructed in relation to Indians and form the fragments of a 'Settler' ethnic identity. I aim to show how changing circumstances in history not only created radically different economies at different times, but also changed the way the Settlers thought about themselves, in relation to one another and in relation to Indians.

The diverse perceptions of the Settlers form part of the contemporary social environment of North West River in that they have currency in different social situations or interactions. Perceptions are aired in conjunction with specific roles, giving rise to a number of 'social characters' in the Settlers' social repertoire. 'Social characters' represent nodes in a volatile social environment, coalescing around perceptions and identities which are grounded in a variety of social experiences. I use the term 'social character,' therefore, to describe the selection by individuals of traits (or perceptions) available and acceptable in their particular social environment, rather than to describe the expression of individual identity. The range of Settler social experience becomes represented by the espousal of different social characters in a variety of situations; and social characters, in turn, become the fluid components of a Settler identity. Each character brings a new set of perceptions to Settler identity, and the espousal of different social characters in different social situations results in the manipulation of that identity. Settler identity is the product of interaction between Settlers as social characters, and, thus, it represents some aspect of this identity in all possible social characters.

In sum, this study concerns itself with the development of the social characters which represent the various aspects of Settler ethnic identity in the community of North West River. This is done by exploring Settler perceptions of Indians and tracing the historical component in the development of these perceptions, with the recognition that historical changes in the social environment of the community have produced the present-day 'bricolage' or patchwork of Settler perceptions.

Two perspectives which attempt to analyse the fragmentation of social identity, and which have not so far been applied to ethnicity, are Goffman's 'frame analysis' (1974) and Rapport's (1983) 'worldviews' of different 'personae' in one individual. Both of these owe much of their theoretical history to phenomenology, linguistics and, particularly, ethnomethodology.

Ethnomethodology (Garfinkel 1952; Schutz 1974) aims at evaluating social meaning and organization from the point of view of the people who form the society. It postulates that people in society are continually making sense of their social environment, and asserts that in order to understand the construction of society it is necessary to study the processes by which members of the society make sense of their social environment. The normally accepted 'superiority' of the reasoning implicit in social scientific theory is denied. 'Commonsense knowledge,' the phrase Schutz used to describe the way people make sense of their social environment, coexists with scientific rationality. Each occupies a different arena, but neither constitutes an exclusive reality. Accepting that there are different methods of viewing the same reality has the effect of fragmenting society into many different realities. Rather than committing itself to one reality, ethnomethodology errs on the side of saying that there is no reality beyond social construction.

The concept of 'commonsense knowledge' describes the way in which Settlers make sense of their society, ethnicity and identity. It also describes, to some extent, the way in which social experience is fragmented for Settlers. Settlers as bricoleurs construct everyday social realities from the remnants of diverse past experiences, and these constructs are then applicable in specific social situations. It is the notion of the fragmentation of social experience that I wish to apply to the study of ethnicity, and this is taken up in two different ways by Goffman and Rapport.

In *Frame Analysis* Goffman divides society into fragments by exploring the contexts, or frames, in which social interaction takes place. Goffman describes how 'frames' are continually being superimposed so that any small fragment of interaction is linked to endless other fragments of interaction.

Rapport, carrying out fieldwork in rural England, analysed conversations between people to show that any one individual was composed of several 'personae' with differing 'worldviews.' In essence, the personae are the fragments of the social world of the people in the village, since each villager was acting in a number of different roles in relation to others.

The extrinsic shaping of social environments selectively encourages the formation of some social characters. 'Frames' and 'personae' are bounded by the social environment, and thus confine the individual to the playing of certain roles and games, thereby limiting the perceptions and responses used. Interactional situations draw upon a stock of perceptions and responses which are embodied in prevailing social characters, rarely without inherent contradictions because of the different social environments from which they arise.

The effects of changing context have been explored only partially in studies of situational ethnicity,[11] but situational ethnicity as described in such studies differs in several important ways from frame, context and personae. Firstly, situational ethnicity describes interaction between two groups rather than within one group. Secondly, it describes ambiguity between ascriptive and achieved statuses rather than considering the possibility that any one individual has access to a number of different social characters simultaneously. Thirdly, it deals with changes and choices as discrete events (which become ends in themselves, such as the taking of sides across ethnic boundaries), rather than continual or multilevelled and reversible swings in a fluid social environment.

Goffman asserts that an individual is involved in several frames at once, and that some of the realities within these frames are contingent upon other realities in other frames. I draw from Goffman's arguments the importance of context and recursive links throughout frames, which, for North West River society, is to explore the historical contexts in which perceptions developed and the present day contexts in which these perceptions come into play. Rapport describes how several personae with distinct worldviews come into play simultaneously, in one conversation. From Rapport, I adopt the idea that people consist of multiple 'personae' in order to show how they are different social characters in different social situations. It is this fluidity in social interaction that I find useful in studying the phenomenon of ethnicity.

The History of European Settlement and Development in the Hamilton Inlet Region

This chapter is a survey of outside influences upon the history of European settlement and development of the Central Labrador region. It is intended to provide the reader with a reservoir of information that will further understanding of ensuing discussions in the book. However, to attempt a history of European settlement in Central Labrador, which covers a period of nearly 250 years, is no small undertaking. This history is complex and extensive, being influenced by events and changes taking place much further afield than Central Labrador, and it has not been exhaustively studied in itself or as part of a more encompassing project. Rather than attempt to produce a comprehensive account of the history of the region, my aim here is to focus attention upon the economic, social and cultural backgrounds which influenced European settlement in Labrador.

The small stream of pioneers arriving in Hamilton Inlet during the late eighteenth and early nineteenth centuries were faced with a frequently hostile, alien environment. These pioneers clung to values and aspirations which had been shaped by their lives in the Old World. The society that developed thus reflected the new Settlers' origins as well as their adaptation to a new environment. They adhered to their old religion and beliefs, such as observing Sunday as a day of rest, and their adherence to religion often gave solace when other social structures had yet to be established:

> I remember that time so well when Father met us at the door as we came home from seeing our rabbit snares, with a book in his hand, and told us she was dying. We all kneeled down near our good mother, breathing her last. By the time Father was done reading and praying, she was gone. Oh, what did I do? Where to go? Far from any other habitation, only five of us, but the Lord was with us (Campbell 1980:24).

The development of the society did not stop with the arrival of pioneers; rather it continually grew and changed as new people arrived in the Inlet. There are recognisable trends in the population history, marked by the arrival of new groups of Settlers with distinct origins and differing reasons for seeking to settle in the Inlet. The history can be divided into three periods: the pioneer period, when settlement was instigated by the Newfoundland fishery; the fur trade period, when settlement was encouraged by the Hudson's Bay Company; and, the administrative period, during which time the International Grenfell Association influenced the sedentarization of the Settler population in Central Labrador. Each of these will be covered in separate sections of the chapter.

THE PIONEER PERIOD: ORIGINS OF THE HAMILTON INLET EUROPEAN POPULATION

Available information on the area indicates that certain families of planters[1] and traders were established around Hamilton Inlet between the late eighteenth and early nineteenth centuries. During this period too, seasonal fishermen, who were brought out to Labrador by merchants and adventurers[2] involved in the Newfoundland fishery, established homes and families in the Inlet rather than returning to Europe or Newfoundland. The lifestyle of the pioneers has been influential in shaping the contemporary culture and society of communities in Hamilton Inlet. Much of the present-day folk history centres around adventures in adapting knowledge from their backgrounds in the Old World to the requisites of their new environment. This section aims to explore the origins of the Settler population in order to understand why the early Settlers emigrated to the New World, and why they ended up in Labrador.

The social history of Hamilton Inlet is fairly well documented from the mid-1830s onwards because of the arrival of the Hudson's Bay Company. However, before the Company opened its North West River post in 1836 there were independent traders and planters living in the area. It is difficult to discover much about these few people who were among the first permanent Settlers in Labrador to come from Europe because documentation is both rare and incomplete. The documents compiled for the Labrador Boundary Dispute occasionally refer to the inhabitants of Hamilton Inlet in the period before the 1830s, but this collection of data is selective and certainly not extensive. The Newfoundland Public Archives has collections of data pertaining to the merchants who had establishments in Labrador. Amongst these are the journals kept by George Cartwright (1792) during his sixteen years in Sandwich Bay, and the crew lists and documents of the Slade and Bird companies.[3] These provide insight into the skills required of crews who intended to winter in Labrador, and the difficulties traders encountered in their pursuit of the fishery.

There are a number of accounts of the lifestyle of the early Settlers compiled by visiting missionaries and officials. The account of the Settlers in Hamilton Inlet, given by Hickson on his visit to assess the need for a Methodist mission for the region in 1824, is typical. His strict Methodist training led him to both pity and condemn the "ungodly Europeans and their Eskimo concubines" (Hickson, in Young 1931:23) with whom he lived during his visit. An accurate portrait of conditions is difficult to draw from such writings. One of the best accounts of pioneer life in the Inlet is given by Lydia Campbell, the daughter of one of the pioneers. Her collection of reminiscences, "Sketches of Labrador Life," was first published as a series of articles in *The Evening Herald* during December and February of 1894 and 1895, and has since been reproduced.

Secondary sources of information pertaining to the period prior to the Hudson's Bay Company's arrival are also scarce. No history of the settlement of Hamilton Inlet has been compiled, and so this account of the history has been gleaned from works which are peripheral in orientation to the subject in hand. Gosling's (1910) history of Labrador deals with Hamilton Inlet in the context of the rest of Labrador. The brief history given by Zimmerly (1975) in his study of the area only sparsely covers this period, and does not discuss the origins of the population, or their social and economic backgrounds. Both Thornton (1977) and Hancock (1977) have studied the settlement trends of people from the West of England who came out with the fishery. Hancock's study concentrates on isolating the towns and villages that supplied most of the Settlers coming to Newfoundland from the West Country, whereas Thornton studies the merchants responsible for settling the Southern Coast of Labrador, which includes the Straits Region and the Southeastern Coast of Labrador. Although neither study deals with Hamilton Inlet Settlers, in combination they describe the trend of settlement on the Southern coast of Labrador instigated by West Country merchants, giving the origins of these first Settlers and the time period and context in which Southeastern Labrador and probably Hamilton Inlet were settled. Matthews (1968a and b) also examines the migration patterns from the Old World during the fishery, and discusses the machinations of the West Country merchants. For an understanding of the conditions in rural England during the pioneer period of migration, I have referred to E. P. Thompson's seminal work, *The Making of the English Working Class* (1978).

A large part of the region's early history will forever remain as the 'Dark Ages' of Labrador because of the limited documentation. Nevertheless, the Settlers who appeared during this period dominate much of the community's oral history, and so are significant to the study.

Newfoundland, and to a lesser extent, the coast of Labrador, had been attracting settlement for a long period prior to the arrival of the first Settlers in Hamilton Inlet. The Newfoundland fishery had attracted Basques as early as the 1500s, and fleets setting sail from the Southwest of England and Northern France had been disputing the right to settle the Island until the signing of the Treaty of Utrecht in 1713. This Treaty was strengthened by further amendments in 1763 (the Treaty of Versailles), and in 1783 the Treaty of Paris gave the lion's share of both Newfoundland and the fishery to Britain.

The Newfoundland fishery was developed by merchants and adventurers from the West of England who had been integral in the discovery of the New World, especially Newfoundland. It was imperative for the West Country merchants to keep business on home territory if they were to retain a strong control of the fishery. To this end, they fought any attempts to settle their portion of the New World. Hence, there was very little settlement anywhere in Newfoundland or Labrador during the seventeenth and most of the eighteenth centuries. However, a greater threat manifested itself in the form of French claims to the region. It became increasingly more apparent that settlement was needed in order to support British claims to the region. In 1765, Palliser, the Governor of Newfoundland, introduced the "Regulations for the coast of Labrador." These instructed that crews of twelve men should be left to winter at fishing posts in order to maintain the facilities that were built each season, and to ward off destructive attacks from foreign opponents. The men normally spent two to three years living in these harbours. Thus began Newfoundland's legitimate 'planter' population. It was not altogether unwelcomed by the merchants because these planters were in an excellent position to make the pursuit of the fishery more efficient.

The Southern Coast of Labrador is shown on the earliest maps of European adventurers and explorers to the New World, and it is this area that became the natural extension to the Newfoundland fishery during the latter half of the eighteenth century. Whilst the discovery of Labrador by the Old World stems back to the Viking era (c.897), and the fishery started a few centuries later with Basque whaling fleets, the various European claims to Labrador were not clarified until the Boundary Dispute of 1927. The first attempts at systematic settlement in Southern Labrador came with the French when the seigneurial system, which existed along the northern shore of the St. Lawrence, extended as far as Red Bay. The first seigneurie, or land grant, was granted in 1702 to Augustine Le Gardeur (Courtemanche), and included Hamilton Inlet (then called Kessesaskion). Courtemanche set up posts only along the southern extreme of his seigneurie, never venturing into Hamilton Inlet. This southern portion was later divided up into smaller concessions most of which were seasonally occupied until 1763 when Labrador was ceded to Britain. By this time the fishery in Newfoundland was thriving, and the coast of Labrador began to join the fishing enterprise of the West Country merchants.

From its beginning the fishery was prone to periodic depressions. During a bad season, it was quite possible for a company to lose all the investments it had made. This served to make the fishery less attractive to those merchants who could afford to compete in more stable commodities. However, the fishery was not short of entrepreneurs. In an atmosphere of increasing competition, it became a matter of great significance whether a company had weathered several seasons and was able to ride a particularly poor season. This ability arose from the security achieved by experience gained and investment made over a period of time.[4]

Several things, then, precipitated the serious settlement of Labrador. The pressing need to establish a more tangible claim to Labrador after the signing of the Treaties of Versailles and Paris was addressed by the vagaries of the Newfoundland fishery itself. In 1790–93, there was a severe depression in the fishery, caused largely by the American Revolutionary war, and later, the Napoleonic wars. Shipping routes were disrupted and the labour force upon which the fishery depended was commandeered to fight in the wars. Because of this particularly severe and drawn-out depression, a number of the West Country merchants became interested in the Labrador fishery. Insecure firms began looking elsewhere for business to bolster their failing enterprises, and the more secure firms among these retreated to Labrador to sit out the depression. Once in Labrador, crews over-wintered rather than risk the hazardous shipping routes and attendant press-gangs. A number of firms extended their businesses from the 'English Shore' of Newfoundland to Labrador. The Dartmouth- and Bristol-linked firm of Noble and

Pinson, whose headquarters were in St. John's, is representative of this movement. As the Newfoundland fishery never fully recovered from the depression, many of these firms eventually retreated permanently to Labrador.

A few other adventurers, driven north earlier because of the competition offered by established merchants further south, had already begun new enterprises in Labrador which were based in England. Cartwright's Bristol-based company was the first recorded establishment in Labrador, at Chateau Bay in 1770. Competition grew as other companies followed Cartwright's initiative. Cartwright responded by moving further north on the Southeastern Coast and opening an establishment at Sandwich Bay, the furthest north any adventurer had dared move because of the somewhat hostile reception expected from the indigenous population. During his sixteen years in Labrador, Cartwright's most steadfast competitors were Noble and Pinson. However, numerous small enterprises came and went during that period.

In 1764 Sir Hugh Palliser, the Governor of Newfoundland, granted land to the Moravian mission in Labrador. This was to have the effect of keeping the northern Inuit away from the fishery in the south, where their raids had been disrupting its progress. The Moravians were also to keep the European fishermen from settling too near the Inuit in the north, in order that these fishermen would not weaken the control the missionaries wished to exercise over the natives. At about the same time, Cartwright was establishing himself in Sandwich Bay. Settlement had apparently already started along the Southern Shore, and was greatly supplemented by hordes of seasonal fishermen in the summer. At this point the first Settlers arrived in Hamilton Inlet.

In her study of mercantile activities along the Southern Coast of Labrador, Patricia Thornton (1977) describes three distinct phases of traders. These are: firstly, the West Country phase, of which Cartwright and Noble and Pinson are the forerunners; secondly, that of the Jersey merchants, such as De Quetteville and Company, who established businesses west of Forteau; and thirdly, the phase when businesses were once again run from the West of England, and included among their recruits workers from the Channel Islands. Two companies were most pertinent to settlement in Hamilton Inlet: Joseph Bird (from Sturminster Newton in Dorset) established a base in Forteau in 1800 and operated a fishing post at Kenimish; and Slade, whose business ran out of Newfoundland as early as 1780s, sent crews up to fish in Groswater Bay.

The reasons why early Settlers wanted to settle permanently in Labrador or Newfoundland, rather than visit seasonally, are obscure. Those wishing to stay in Newfoundland and Labrador in order to be nearer the fishery had to weigh the convenience of being close to the industry against the hostile winter climate and isolation from food or any kind of service. Abject poverty or political problems at home often tipped the balance in favour of permanent settlement in the New World, despite the attempts of the English merchants to prevent it.

During the mid-eighteenth century, when wintering in Labrador began, Britain was in a state of turmoil, due to the American and Napoleonic wars and to economic changes affecting her agriculture and industry. The movement towards enclosure, which lasted from the mid-eighteenth century until well into the nineteenth century, changed the face of Britain's countryside by enclosing the inefficient strips and common grazing land into large fields in privately owned farms. England had had a dense rural population before the enclosures. Along with the Industrial Revolution, the enclosures effectively transformed the country's population from a rural to an urban one. To avoid starvation, those who could left rural areas for the towns. However, many of the towns during this period were also forced to cope with the surplus workers caused by the advance of technology in industry which rendered many types of craft production obsolete. The West of England textile industry was severely affected by industrial advance, and so the towns and villages of Dorset, Wilt-shire and Devon yielded a goodly crop of aspiring emigrants to the merchants in search of labour for their fishing establishments in Labrador.

The first Settlers who ventured as far north as Hamilton Inlet were, in many cases, avoiding the press gangs which sought men to crew ships for the American and French conflicts; they found it preferable to stay in Labrador and try to make good rather than risk remaining at home. Under the press gangs, whole fishing crews were pirated and men seeking work in ports were impressed into crews for war ships. Merchants with establishments in Newfoundland remained in Newfoundland rather than risk their vessels and crews in returning to England. Many sailors jumped ship and stayed in North America, a few making their way as far north as Labrador.

As with the first Newfoundland planters, the men who came out to work in Labrador stayed for three or four winters before returning home. Presumably, men were rehired from year to year, much as Cartwright describes in his journal. He often re-hired men who had spent a season in his employ, and not infrequently he hired those who had just left another firm. This meant that employees must have spent a good deal longer living in Labrador than any individual contract would suggest. Men employed to spend the winter in Labrador were not just fishing crews. Merchants who opened new establishments needed men to maintain them—builders, carpenters, bricklayers, sawyers, blacksmiths, coopers, masons and the like, as well as boatbuilders and fishermen. Cartwright soon had furriers on his payroll at Sandwich Bay to extend his trapping activities. A number of the trades of the first generation of Settlers are recorded on the headstones in graveyards along the Southern Coast of Labrador (Thornton 1977:165).

Cartwright also began bringing women out as maids, housekeepers and cooks. Both Thornton and Hancock point out as significant the fact that women were introduced to the various establishments. Settlement occurs only when a part of the migrant population decides to remain permanently, raising families in the area. This can happen only when women form part of the population. At the same time, Cartwright not infrequently describes in his journal the liaisons formed between his workers and native women living at one or other of his establishments.

The Labrador Settlers came from the hinterlands of the ports where vessels called to recruit labour on their way to the New World. In Cartwright's time these would have been Dartmouth, Bristol, Cork and Waterford, and later, London as well.[5] De Quetteville drew labour from the Channel Islands during the 1780s and 90s.[6] But a majority of the Settlers came out during the time that Joseph Bird and Slade were establishing their companies in Southern Labrador. Recruitment for Bird's was mainly from the Dorset villages and towns just north of Blackmore Vale and following the Stour valley (Thornton 1977; Hancock 1977), and recruitment for Slade's was from the ports and inland villages of South Devon.[7]

There were both planters and traders among the people already settled in Hamilton Inlet in 1836. In his account of the history of the region, Zimmerly names two Englishmen who are recognized in oral history as being the first men to settle in Hamilton Inlet. These men, Phippard and Newhook, are thought to have arrived in Hamilton Inlet at around 1788. Although they married Inuit women from the Inlet, they left no descendants. Shortly after them, in the early 1790s, Ambrose Brooks arrived from Brighton on the south coast of England. Brooks married an orphaned Inuk who had run away from her community. Many of the residents of North West River trace their ancestry back to this couple and their family (see Chapter Four).

The names of two traders appear in the 1836 Hudson's Bay Journal (McGrath 1927) as being established in Hamilton Inlet. Thomas Groves was mentioned as a trader with his own establishment at Tubb Harbour, on the Southeastern Coast of Labrador, and it was noted that he was willing to loan buildings to the Hudson's Bay men. The name Groves exists in both Sandwich Bay and Hamilton Inlet. Joseph Bird's company was also mentioned. He ran a salmon fishing post at Kenimish, which is still inhabited, across the bay from the present site of North West River. Bird's operations in Labrador began in 1810 (Thornton 1977).

References are made in the folk history of North West River both to the rural life in England which had been forsaken by the pioneers of Hamilton Inlet, and to the Napoleonic wars. In her diary, Lydia Campbell remembers her father, Ambrose Brooks, reminiscing about the life he left in England:

> When I first remember to see things and to understand, I thought there was no place as good as this in the world, and that my father and mother and my two sisters was the best in the world; but our good father used to take me on his knee and tell me his home was a better country, only it was hard to live there after his good old father died and his mother could not keep him so he stayed with a good old minister, that was living in the parish, until he died, and then he came out to this country to try his fortune in this place, for the wars was raging between England and France and all over the world and the pressgangs were pressing the young men, so he and a lot more English people came out up the shore for woodcutters, seal fishing and the cod fishery, which was the highest in those days (Campbell 1980:7-8).

Edna Campbell, a contemporary North West River resident, remembers songs she learnt from her great uncle, Eamon Chaulk, dating back to the Napoleonic wars. The relative freedom of pioneer life in Labrador, the unlimited land and abundant game, must have seemed marvellous to the early Settlers, and must have gone a long way towards compensating them for the isolation and the harsh new environment they had to face.

THE FUR TRADE PERIOD: HISTORY OF THE HUDSON'S BAY COMPANY INVOLVEMENT IN NORTH WEST RIVER

With the arrival of the Hudson's Bay Company, documentation increases, this gives a more complete picture of the social development of North West River. The society which evolved was dependent upon two main components, one of which was the social structure of the Hudson's Bay Company and the other, the labour force itself which was recruited from the Orkney Islands in Scotland. A survey of these elements is a prerequisite to describing adequately the growth of the community of North West River in this period.

Goldring (1980) gives an excellent analysis of the working structure of the Hudson's Bay Company after its amalgamation with the North West Company. Although the book is primarily concerned with recruitment and employment patterns for Rupert's Land (central Canada), the general structure and practices described for the Northern Department apply equally for other departments such as the Montreal Department, in which North West River is located.

There are few studies of the relationship between Orkney and the Hudson's Bay Company. J. Storer Clouston wrote a series of three articles in *The Beaver* between 1936 and 1937, but these are more descriptive than analytical. The most recent and informative study is John Nicks' essay 'Orkneymen in the HBC 1790–1821' (1980). His study concentrates on the recruits from one parish in Orkney (Orphir) over a period of thirty years, between 1790 and 1821. The economic and social history of Orkney itself is covered in numerous studies.[8]

The Hudson's Bay Company Journals for Rigolet and North West River for the period 1834–1910 constitute the main primary source of information about Hamilton Inlet during that time. I have used the copies of the Journals found among the papers compiled by Sir Patrick McGrath for Newfoundland's case in the Labrador boundary dispute of 1927.[9] These are supplemented by articles in *The Beaver*, and also by the records, when they were kept, of independent traders who were in the region at the same time. There are also a few personal diaries and reminiscences, kept intermittently by the early Settlers. However, these personal recollections do not in themselves build an accurate picture of the history of the Inlet because they are so limited. The Company Journals, which focus on the daily activities in and around the posts, describe events and mention the names of people and places. Yet they are unavoidably biased with regard to what records were kept and in the way in which information is recorded. Even taking this bias into account, the wealth of information offered by these records is extremely useful. The Journals represent one of the few consistent and detailed forms of recorded history for the region.

A charter issued from London in 1670 gave the Hudson's Bay Company exclusive trading rights in the area around Hudson's Bay, but the control of trade over such a vast area proved difficult from the beginning. French merchants had been trading in the area prior to 1670 and independent traders continued to carry on with their business after the establishment of the Hudson's Bay Company. Hudson's Bay Company managers in charge of inland posts were required to be resourceful because they had little communication with other posts or head offices between the seasonal visits of boats bringing merchandise and new recruits. A structure developed within the Hudson's Bay Company which enabled its traders to cope both with the competition and with the isolation the posts faced in the early years of operation in the north. The structure depended on loyalty from Company workers and the establishment of hierarchies and class-based social structures. Since the latter were based on the British class system, they ensured that gentlemen[10] and servants fresh to the north knew how to respond to each other despite the unfamiliar conditions in which they found themselves. The hierarchy developed into a system unique to the Hudson's Bay Company, one that absorbed new recruits and, in the beginning, gave enough incentives to all ranks to establish a sense of loyalty.

The main hierarchical structure divided the Hudson's Bay Company employees into gentlemen and servants (or officers and workers). Gentlemen and servants were drawn from very different backgrounds in Britain. Gentlemen were almost exclusively recruited through the London office. They were required to be literate, as maintaining accounts and keeping records were part of their duties. Shareholders, as one of their privileges, had the right to bestow apprenticeships where they saw fit, and, although these favours were "not tossed around indiscriminately" (Goldring 1980: 50), family connections often helped. Servants, on the other hand, were recruited through regional offices, such as the one in Stromness, Orkney. The difference between the origins of the gentlemen and the servants helped to perpetuate the hierarchy.

Gentlemen, who were recruited from social classes in which their position was recognized, also expected to be treated as gentlemen when they arrived in the north.[11]

> Rank brought privileges. Those which set a man's relations to the Hudson's Bay Company and its property were spelled out. Those which fixed his relations with subordinates lay among the tangled skein of unwritten traditions of the service (Goldring 1980:58).

The gentlemen were set apart from the servants by obvious differences in lifestyle—such as different tasks, food allowances and more leisure time—as well as by more subtle differences such as in the control of information and authority. Being transferred to other posts without notice was more common among servants than gentlemen. Gentlemen were also shareholders; traders being entitled to half shares, and factors to a full share, while ordinary workers were given wages.

The need for skilled workers grew as the Company consolidated its pattern of expansion. A majority of the recruits required by the Hudson's Bay Company were ordinary labourers, but a significant number of tradesmen were needed at the main posts. The production of tools, building and repairing of boats, construction and maintenance of post buildings and the collection of wood for fuel and building were common tasks at all posts. Workers were increasingly expected to supplement their food allowances, and often had to supply meat or fish for the post in which they lived. Some posts began gardening and farming on a small scale in order to give variety to employees' diets. North West River became famous for the gardens, cultivated under Factor Donald Smith's management, which produced a range of basic vegetables and hay for a number of livestock. Hunting, fishing and the tending of gardens and livestock, then, became work requirements. In North West River the workers also trapped when they had the opportunity, and newly released employees who had chosen to stay in the region became the Company's fur suppliers.

Some kinds of tradesmen were more commonly employed than others. Among the most common were boatbuilders, carpenters, sawyers, coopers and other woodworkers, and, in the earlier years, stonemasons. Less common but essentially more valuable tradesmen were the blacksmiths and tinsmiths who made traps, ice chisels, horseshoes, knives, and anything from bedsteads to nails. (The contingent of men arriving at North West River in 1836 included carpenters and a blacksmith.) The different trades gave rise to an informal hierarchy within the ranks of servants. Blacksmiths were often recruited from urban rather than rural areas where they were more likely to have had the benefit of some education. They tended to gain the respect of all the other workers, often becoming the spokesmen for the servant class as a whole because the value of their skills put them in a relatively secure position. The more prestigious tradesmen had a longstanding argument with the Company because they refused to do ordinary labouring, preferring to carry out only the functions of their trades. However, the Hudson's Bay Company needed, above all, a versatile work force, and tradesmen had limited specific functions which were periodically essential, but which did not fill all their time. When retired employees began to settle, the Company was able to employ them as tradesmen on a seasonal or temporary basis. In North West River, for instance, Daniel Campbell was seasonally employed as a cooper, and gained a certain amount of prestige because of his ability to fulfill this necessary function. But until this was the case, the Company required that all their workers carry out any task that had to be done.

The Hudson's Bay Company has a long history of recruiting its workers from Orkney. The Orkney port of Stromness was a convenient stopping place for the Company ships leaving London and sailing north along the eastern seaboard of Britain. The port offered fresh water, supplies and labour to passing ships. The whaling fleets headed for the Davis Straits also recruited men from Stromness.[12] Perhaps more significant was what the Hudson's Bay Company offered to the Orcadians.

Orkney has always been agriculturally oriented, but the various systems of land ownership and tenure had caused farming to be inefficient until the advent of enclosure. The English absentee landlords, who owned and controlled large tracts of agricultural land, first introduced enclosure during the 1760s. Many small tenants were dispossessed, and life for the majority of people in Orkney became extremely unpleasant. There were few labouring jobs available on the enclosed farms, and wages for these jobs were low. And yet, these early enclosures did little to change the inefficiency of farming in Orkney. At the turn of the eighteenth century, then, Orkney had very little money and few opportunities for people to improve their standard of living above mere subsistence level. A popular alternative form of employment was offered by the Hudson's Bay Company, which recruited young, able-bodied men to work in the New World.

The kelp industry in Orkney began in 1722, and increasingly employed people from the crofts and cottages, when their land could not provide subsistence. The industry lasted for over a century, collapsing suddenly in 1832 when the removal of tariffs permitted the importation of European seaweed at much lower prices. This left people suddenly out of work and with little opportunity to go back to a land-based economy. Many people left Orkney, and again, the Hudson's Bay Company offered a means by which to leave for greener pastures.

The wages offered by the Hudson's Bay Company in 1790 (the peak period of recruitment from Orkney) varied considerably, depending upon the skills and trades of the employees. For a basic labourer the wage was between £6 and £8 a year. A boat-builder earned between £20 and £30, and a house carpenter earned as

much as £36. At the same time rural workers in Orkney earned
between £2.10 and £3.10 in a full year of employment, providing
that there was work. (Nicks 1980:117). This in itself was enough
incentive for some of the destitute population, but signing up for a
stipulated period of assured employment also offered security. The
Hudson's Bay Company provided for all basic needs of its workers
as well; passage, food, lodgings and a minimum of clothing. This,
and the fact that there was little to spend money on in the wilds of
Canada, meant that the employees were able to save much of their
income over the period in which they were employed. Many saved
enough to set themselves up as farmers on their return.[13] With their
savings, these returned workers acquired a certain notoriety in
Orkney. Whether they returned to farming or not, their wealth
effectively raised their social status as long as their savings lasted.
(Sometimes servants returned home only to sign up again for a
second term after a short period in Orkney.)

The northern way of life also had appeal because of its relative
freedom from social constraints, and it was not uncommon for
servants to form liaisons with local Labradorians. Social pressures
at home might also have resulted in extending sojourns in the North
West, as one of the ministers in the *Old Statistical Account* mentions:

> When a man and his wife cannot live in peace together, the parties
> and the parish are relieved from such disquiets, by the husband's
> retreat to the Hudson's Bay settlements (Sinclair 1927:120–1).

Such was the success of recruiting workers in Orkney that at
the end of the eighteenth century 78 percent of all Hudson's Bay
Company employees were from the Islands. The Company employed
between sixty and a hundred men each season, and at the peak of
this relationship an average recruitment was seventy men. The
Reverend William Clouston, in the *Old Statistical Account*, said that
the Hudson's Bay Company preferred these 'Orkney men' because
they were "more sober and tractable than the Irish, and they engage
for lower wages than either the English or the Irish" (Sinclair
1927:148). Perhaps the fewer alternatives open to Orcadians provided the Hudson's Bay Company with a better choice of recruits
than it could find elsewhere. The remaining 22 percent were almost
entirely in the officer category, and from England (Nicks 1980:
102).[14]

The situation changed in the nineteenth century. While improve-
ments in farming had been made gradually since the 1790s, when
a few landowners had enclosed their farms successfully, it was not
until after 1830 that most of Orkney was transformed from a region

of uneconomical land use and poor management to one of the most productive agricultural regions in Scotland. In the latter half of the nineteenth century, the arable acreage increased by 250 percent in Orkney, and from the 1830s onwards, the economy and standard of living in Orkney improved by leaps and bounds. It was after the 1830s that interest in working for the Hudson's Bay Company declined.

Poor communications in the eighteenth century limited travel between parishes in Orkney, and so most of the early recruits were drawn from parishes which bordered Stromness. Nicks[15] calculated that approximately a quarter of the recruits hired before the amalgamation of the Hudson's Bay Company with the North West Company in 1821 came regularly from one of the poorer social groups, that which was formed by the crofters. Nicks' study of the pre-amalgamation period also reveals that patronage influenced much of the recruitment, either from family members already successfully employed by the company or from prestigious figures in the community such as the priest and school teacher.[16] Clouston (1937) follows the fortunes of a group of recruits hired in 1798 and says that "fully two-thirds bore the names of one-time land-owning families, and fourteen of these were even numbered once among the 'best landed men' found on the assizes of the sixteenth century head courts" (p. 40).

This finding may help to explain the change in the quality of recruits that the Hudson's Bay Company clerks noted after amalgamation. The Company found that the 'quality' of the Orkney men had dropped and now workers were no longer 'loyal and industrious' but 'sly,' 'slothful' and even 'unable to carry out the tasks required of them.' Goldring (1980) describes recruits after 1821 as coming from the "lower levels of society, from families with too little land, trade or influence to share with the rising generation" (p. 178). However, as we shall see below, it is more likely that the responsibility for the differences in the calibre of workers hired after amalgamation lies with the changes made in the Hudson's Bay Company's own hiring policies, rather than the personal history of its workers.

A combination of factors resulted in a decline in the number of Orkney men working for the Hudson's Bay Company after the turn of the century. The needs of the Company had changed, as had circumstances in Orkney. In 1821 the Hudson's Bay Company absorbed the old North West Company. Amalgamation caused a surfeit of employees and recruitment was cut back. This was primarily due to the fact that the Hudson's Bay Company inherited a local supply of workers, namely the French-speaking Canadian[17] employees of the former North West Company. The Hudson's Bay Company wages also stagnated against the improving rates of pay for labour in Orkney. This stagnation was compounded by the tendency of the Company's hierarchy to become more rigid after amalgamation. Whereas before, opportunities had existed for ardent workers to make careers for themselves in the Company, now there was little opportunity left for ordinary servants to make good and rise through the ranks. Thus contracts with the Company became less and less appealing.

Re-engagement was one tactic used by the Hudson's Bay Company to maintain an optimal supply of efficient workers; it was also the one single change in policy that most enhanced settlement. Under normal circumstances it was the Company's policy to discourage its employees from settling permanently. It is significant that the tendency to re-engage began during the time that the Company was expanding into Labrador, since long term re-engagement frequently encouraged settlement there.

Re-engagement became more expedient as the Company encountered difficulties in recruiting from outside. It saved the Company from having to find, train and transport new recruits. However, the Company's unwillingness to increase its wages caused difficulties for the traders and factors who needed ways of enticing their good workers to stay. The Company preferred to rehire workers at the same rate of pay, while new incoming recruits received slightly better wages. Despite this, re-engagement was often the only recourse for desperately under-staffed posts. Post managers found ways of promoting desirable workers, either by raising them from the rank of labourer to that of craftsman, or by creating categories of work which then required promotion. Categories such as boat-builder, fisherman and mechanic were used in this way, allowing for a change in title but not necessarily a change in duties. In fact, Governor Simpson described his labour supply as turning over approximately every nine years. As this represents close to the term of two contract periods, a fair number of employees must have been regularly re-hired.[18]

When recruiting from Orkney became difficult, the Hudson's Bay Company began recruiting elsewhere, notably from Lower Canada and the Red River settlement. Two French Canadians who found their way to the North West River post in the 1830s, and a Scandinavian recruit who arrived in the 1850s are possible examples of the Company's recruiting experiments. The Company did not find enough suitable recruits, however, until the collapse of the kelp industry in Orkney in 1832 again created a dire need for work with the Hudson's Bay Company. This coincided with a period of expansion by the Company, which was now secure in its monopoly of trade in the north.

Despite low wages, a considerable proportion of the Hudson's Bay Company's workers came from Orkney during the 1830s and, in 1836, the complement of men arriving in Hamilton Inlet to set up the post at North West River were Orkneymen. The wealth and freedom of Hamilton Inlet in comparison to the conditions that they had left in Orkney must have seemed overwhelming to the first recruits to the North West River post. Lydia Campbell describes the richness of wildlife in the Inlet just before the start of the fur trade with the Hudson's Bay Company:

> About this time people began to settle, one after another, mostly French people, few English, for everything was plentiful at that time. People could stand on the rocks and hook fish ashore on the beach and spear the salmon that was swimming along the shore. I heard Father say that people could not row up and down the river with any tide, they would have to wait until the tide would turn for to clear the fish and caplin away before they could row through them. Everything was so plentiful (1980:17).

Labrador was one of the regions into which the Hudson's Bay Company was extending its domain during the late 1820s and 1830s. The potential of starting a post at North West River was seen by Erland Erlandson, a Hudson's Bay Company employee who had recently opened the Fort Chimo post in Ungava Bay. In 1834, Erlandson was crossing the interior of Labrador on his way from Fort Chimo to Mingan on the North Shore of Quebec. He was taken to North West River instead of Mingan by his Indian guides. On his return to Fort Chimo he reported that there were already traders in Hamilton Inlet, and he recommended that the Company establish posts there. In 1836 a contingent of men under the auspices of Simon McGillivray set out from the 'King's Posts'[19] to establish a post at North West River:

> The Governor and Committee have determined on meeting the opposition that has recently been commenced at Esquimaux Bay by Stuart of Quebec, acting, it is said, for himself, and on behalf of some people in Boston, United States, with the view of encroaching on our Trade with the Mingan Indians and anticipating us in the occupation of the back country situated between Esquimaux and Ungava Bays and to that end an expedition consisting of Mr McGillivray—the gentleman appointed to the charge thereof—two clerks and twelve men is to be fitted out this season with sufficient

quantity of Trading Goods, Provisions &c which you will forward
as early in the Season as possible say in the course of the month
of May in a vessel to be chartered by Mr James McKenzie. Of the
Servants to be employed on this expedition, I am desirous that four
should be Orkney men and eight Canadians. The Orkney-men you
can either get at Mingan or in the King's Posts, of those to be
brought out this season whose wages are 17 pounds per ann. for
five years, and the Canadians, Middlemen or common voyagers you
will engage if possible at the same wages for the term of 3 years. It
is desirable a good fisherman should be of the party; likewise one
or two rough carpenters and a Blacksmith, and it will be necessary
that the Expedition should be provided with netts and Tools for the
Tradesmen (extract of a letter from George Simpson to John Siev-
right, 1836. In McGrath 1927, box 11, folder 6, p. 25–26).[20]

Among the number of small traders in Hamilton Inlet at this time
was Joseph Bird of Forteau, who came to Labrador in 1810. Bird
was still operating a salmon fishery at Kenimish and keeping a
winter house in Shabis Kasho (Sebaskachu). Both the salmon post
and the winter house were sold to the Hudson's Bay Company for
£40 soon after the latter arrived. On his way to Hamilton Inlet,
McGillivray met with a Captain Lock, who was employed by Bird,
and purchased Bird's business in the region through him:

A Brig (Hope) belonging to Mr Bird of Forteau and a French
schooner cast anchor among us. This Mr Bird has an establishment
in Esqx. Bay called Kinimish... [I] made some arrangements wt.
Capt. Lock of the Hope (Agent for Mr Bird) to purchase Kinimish.
He offers the premises for 40 Cy. [pounds] but I must first see the
place. ...

Purchased the stores and premises about here from Capt. Lock,
agent for Mr (Thos) Bird of Forteau, for the sum of 40 Cy. [pounds]
for which I gave him a draft on the Hudson's Bay house in London.
There is a winter house also at Shabis Kasho, halfway, between
this & Moolagen, which is included in this bargain. (McGillivray
writing in the Hudson's Bay Company Journal for North West River
in 1836. In McGrath 1927, box 12, folder 1, p. 2 and 10).

Another trader in the region, Thomas Groves, was also willing to
sell property to the Hudson's Bay Company. He gave them a house
at a place now called Groves Point, in the region of Goose Bay, and
sold them his shares in "a fine masted large boat called the Race
Horse" (ibid, p. 4). Groves, however, unlike Bird, continued to trade
in the region, his main post being at Tubb Harbour on the coast.[21]
The task of the first recruits was to construct the buildings for
the post in the face of the hostilities of the other traders already
established in the region. Comeau, the North West River agent for

the Boston trader Stewart, gave the early Hudson's Bay Company recruits a difficult time. The Company's policy was to compete for trade directly with an opponent, and this involved building a post upstream from the opponent in order to lure the Indians first as they came out of the interior. If the opponents retaliated by themselves moving further upstream, the Hudson's Bay Company workers were expected to follow suit until the opponent conceded defeat. Apparently Comeau not only moved his posts with alacrity but he also offered alcohol to those Indians whose trade he sought. The Hudson's Bay Company did not allow the distribution of alcohol to Indians at the time. It took considerable time to organize the construction of post buildings because of the fierce competition Comeau gave the Hudson's Bay Company men, and in low spirits towards the end of the summer, McGillivray described the expedition as "a voyage of disappointment throughout" (ibid, p. 8).

The arrival of the Hudson's Bay Company in Hamilton Inlet had its effect on the small Settler population which was already established. These Settlers had been making use of several diverse ecological niches and learning skills from the indigenous Inuit and Indian peoples who occupied complementary littoral and inland environments. The native population was prominent in the early years, but as time went by they were affected in various ways by the influx of Europeans. Smallpox had earlier wiped out most of the Inuit population below Hamilton Inlet, and the establishment of the Moravian missions at Hopedale and Nain drew the remainder of the population away from Hamilton Inlet. Zimmerly (1975:72) speculates that the Settlers' habit of marrying Inuit women depleted the number of eligible wives for Inuit men in the south so much so that this also became a reason for the latter to migrate north. Elsner, the Moravian missionary who visited the Inlet at the behest of the Hudson's Bay Company Factor Donald Smith to estimate the need for a mission there, commented on the population of the bay thus: "On Esquimaux-Bay, and its coves, in a district about 150 miles long, there are to be found twenty-one fishermen's families, and, at the outside, not more than ten families of Esquimaux" (Elsner 1857:448). The Indian population increasingly kept to the interior as the coast and Inlet waterways became settled, and their visits to the coast became limited to the summer, when they came to the trading posts.

For various reasons, then, European contact with these indigenous peoples had resulted in their retreat to the north and west, leaving the Central Labrador basin predominantly occupied by Settlers. This led to an unusual situation for the Hudson's Bay

Company. The normal pattern for the Company to adopt when establishing a new region was to import the management and labour requirements for its own posts and rely on the local population, usually Indians, to supply these posts with furs. In Labrador this was almost impossible from the outset because the indigenous population was small and had largely withdrawn from the region. Those who did come out to the posts were not reliable fur suppliers, partly because they were not sufficiently attracted to the goods and services offered by the posts to become dependent on such goods. In the area to the north of Hamilton Inlet this was partly caused by the fact that they would have to forsake hunting caribou in order to trap furs, since the ecological areas required for the two activities were very different. Research on the Naskapi of the 'Barren Grounds' shows how manipulation by the Hudson's Bay Company brought about dependence on trade goods and resulted in starvation amongst the Indians (Cooke 1979; Henriksen 1973). The Hudson's Bay Company encouraged a reliance on guns and ammunition so that the Naskapi had to trap fur in return for the ammunition they needed in order to hunt. This eventually led to a precarious division of time spent hunting in one area and trapping in another. The Naskapi were left destitute when the caribou migration path changed, taking the herds too far away for the Indians to reach. Looking through the post's journals it becomes obvious that the Indians did not initially bring in much fur, and never became major fur suppliers:

> They [Indians] generally went in the winter and killed a sufficient number of Beaver, Otter, and Marten in this track to purchase a stock of necessary articles such as guns, tobacco and ammunition; and, after their return hither, in the following summer, never thought of hunting a skin until their necessities obliged them to start again for the above mentioned posts [King's Posts] ... (extract of a letter from Nicol Finlayson, Hudson's Bay Company Factor at Fort Chimo, 1834. In McGrath 1927, box 11, folder 6, p. 10–11).

Finlayson is referring here to the Naskapi who roamed between the North Shore of Quebec, Labrador and Ungava.

The Hudson's Bay Company, wanting a more committed trapping force, had to find alternative fur suppliers for their Labrador posts. They turned to the Settler population, which grew increasingly as retiring recruits chose to remain and settle in the region. At the outset there were too few Settlers to bring in many furs, and the Company used its own labour force to supply the posts with furs, cutting and maintaining traplines along the river system:

Immediately after the business of the summer season is closed by the departure of the vessel, generally about the middle of September, the men are sent in parties of two each, up the different rivers, to pass the winter in trapping martens and other animals; they live in small huts, warmed by a stove; their work consists in visiting their traps, keeping them free from snow, and in hunting for a part of their subsistence. ...The men, on leaving the main Post, are furnished with a certain quantity of pork, flour, and ammunition, which is expected to last them until they return in the spring, generally about the first or second week in June (Davies 1843:87–8).

However, it became much more economical for the Company if the labourers ceased to be the responsibility of the Hudson's Bay Company in a credit and debit system. Therefore settlement was encouraged here, unlike other parts of the continent where it was actively discouraged. At the end of their contracts many of the retiring recruits settled in the region, rather than risk returning to the poverty-stricken Orkneys, thus becoming the major fur suppliers for the Company.

Workers arriving with the Hudson's Bay Company brought some useful skills and trades. The Company records for the time list 'tin-men' (tinsmiths), blacksmiths and boat-builders amongst others, and some of these craftsmen settled in the area. Having resident craftsmen in the local population meant that the Company could hire them seasonally as the need arose. The case of Daniel Campbell is an example. He was hired by the Hudson's Bay Company in 1845 as a cooper, a trade that was essential to the transporting of salmon from the region. He later married Ambrose Brooks' daughter, Lydia, and became an independent trapper, but he was available to work as a cooper for the Company when they needed one, as his daughter Margaret describes in her diary: "Sometime in March, Mr. Smith [the Hudson's Bay Company factor] sent for Father, for he was the only cooper in the bay. He wanted him for a month to get some barrels ready for the spring" (Baikie 1976:31). Lydia Campbell's sister Hannah was also seasonally employed by the Company to prepare winter clothing for the recruits when they first arrived.

It was primarily Donald Smith, factor at Rigolet and North West River from 1848 until 1868, who was responsible for the development of an efficient trapping and salmon fishing economy in Central Labrador under the aegis of the Hudson's Bay Company. He had begun his career by managing the King's Posts which were situated along the North Shore of Quebec. Shortly after his arrival in

Labrador he became trader, and then factor (in 1852) of the Central
Labrador posts. Under his management North West River became
the regional centre, and the post was expanded to include roads,
gardens and a small number of livestock such as cattle, horses and
chickens. The explorer, Hallock, described the effect of coming upon
this 'farm' in the middle of Labrador:

> Then the astonished ear is greeted with the lowing of cattle and the
> bleeting of sheep on shore; and in the rear of the agent's house are
> veritable barns, from whose open windows hangs fragrant new-
> mown hay; and a noisy cackle within is ominous of fresh-laid eggs!
> Surely Nature has been remarkably lavish here, or some presiding
> genius, of no ordinary enterprise and taste, has redeemed the place
> from its wilderness desolation! Both are true. The climate is much
> warmer here than upon the coast, and there is a fair admixture of
> soil. Donald Alexander Smith, the intelligent Agent of the post, is
> a practical farmer, and, by continued care and the employment of
> proper fertilizing agents, succeeds in forcing to maturity, within the
> short summer season, most of the vegetables and grains produced
> in warmer latitudes. He has seven acres under cultivation, of which
> a considerable portion is under glass. There are growing turnips,
> pease, cucumbers, potatoes, pumpkins, melons, cauliflowers, bar-
> ley, oats, etc. Corn will not ripen, nor even form upon the ear. Before
> Smith's house is a flower-garden. Here, too, is a carriage road two
> miles long (strange sight in this roadless country!), upon which the
> agent betimes indulges in the luxury of a drive; for he has two
> horses which he employs upon the farm. A bull, twelve cows, half
> a dozen sheep, goats, fowls, and dogs comprise his live-stock. There
> is no other place like Smith's in Labrador, in all its area of 420,000
> square miles! (Hallock 1861: 758–9).

Smith's farm provided much of the food requirements of the
posts under his control. Most Hudson's Bay Company posts had to
rely upon the annual arrival of goods shipped in at considerable cost
from Britain. Supplies of dried goods such as flour, rice, and some
dried fruit were severely limited, and often preserved delicacies were
rancid on arrival. Rather than allow the exigencies of shipping to
circumscribe the diet of his staff, Smith was able to provide fresh
and varied foodstuffs to supplement the fish and wild meats his men
hunted. There are numerous references in the post journals to the
planting, tending and harvesting activities of the North West River
recruits.

Smith also fully exploited the salmon fishery which had been
started by the early traders such as Louis Fornel, Joseph Bird,
Thomas Groves and the North Westers, Stewart and Comeau. The
increasing turnover at the posts as he developed the salmon fishery

and other resources had the effect of drawing out and directing the activities of the Inlet population, since most of the population became employed either directly or indirectly by the Hudson's Bay Company. Smith was an extremely enterprising man, but the stamina and work required by these enterprises were not altogether appreciated by the Hudson's Bay Company: "We are all sadly overworked here, our business is increasing each season, yet we have the same number of labourers and we are not expected to increase our expenses," wrote Smith from Rigolet in 1856 (Willson 1915:129). This situation reflects the difficulties that the Hudson's Bay Company were experiencing in recruitment.

Smith was responsible for introducing to Labrador the practice of canning salmon for commercial retail. This was particularly insightful since commercial canning was a recent innovation, and it remained a successful industry long after Smith's retirement from the region:

> I have worked like a slave since I have been here, and like yourself I am glad to say that my tough labours have been crowned with success. The collection of salmon at this post alone amounts to 370 tierces[22] against 95 sent to the London market last outfit. At Cartwright, in Sandwich Bay, there are ready for shipment 360 tierces; from these two places alone we ship 730, against 401 packages sent to London last year, including Ungava and other northern sections. If Ungava does its quota, we should ship between 11 and 1200 tierces. (Chief Factor P. W. Bell writing in the 1864 Hudson's Bay Company Journal for North West River. In McGrath 1927, box 12, folder 1).

Tinsmiths became regular members of the parties of recruits arriving annually at the Rigolet and North West River posts. The introduction of canning may have been the major cause of the growth and success of the salmon fishery in Labrador after Smith's arrival. Previously, there had been no way of transporting salmon the distances required to reach large markets.

Smith must have demanded a lot from his men in adding fishing and farming to their workloads, and in exacting labour from an insufficiently large staff during these days of expansion. However he also gave a great deal of his time and energies to the Hamilton Inlet populace, of whom, by this time, a fair number had formerly been Orkney recruits for his posts and nearly all were working on some level for the Company. He practised rudimentary medicine, and acted as judge and arbiter in disputes. He even served instead of a priest in marriage and baptism ceremonies for the Settler population.

Donald Smith left Labrador in 1868 for Montreal where he became Governor of the Hudson's Bay Company, not long after the death of Sir George Simpson. Before his departure, he had succeeded in putting Labrador firmly on the Hudson's Bay Company map. By the time he left, there was a thriving population of Settlers in Hamilton Inlet, with North West River undisputedly at the centre. As the post developed and more recruits became Settlers, the main salmon fishing posts and traplines changed hands. Whereas formerly they had been run by Hudson's Bay Company staff, now they were run by independent Settlers. Reference is made to Traverse Pine (Traverspine), a trapline following the Traverspine River, which changed hands from the Company to John Goudie and family (and back again when the family decided to move north). Kenimish, a salmon fishing post, is also mentioned. Malcolm Maclean and Henry Hay initially ran the post as Hudson's Bay Company employees, and later independently.[23]

The Blakes, Groves and Meshers of the pioneering period were gradually supplemented by Michelins, Goudies, Campbells, Baikies, McLeans and Montagues over the next sixty years, as the Company's Orkney recruits became independent Settlers. Retiring Hudson's Bay Company recruits were not only responsible for a major growth in the Hamilton Inlet population from the end of the nineteenth century until the Depression, they were also instrumental in shaping the Settlers' lifestyle in that period, primarily through example. Davies' description of the activities of the Hudson's Bay Company workers (see earlier) soon became the template for the Settler seasonal cycle, in which trapping was the major activity. The economy of the Lake Melville region changed from the seasonal fluctuation between littoral fishing and inland trapping orientations of the pioneer Settlers — the isolated families of "frolicksome sailors who prefer[ed] the freedom of a semi-barbarous life and the society of a brown squaw to the severity of maritime discipline and the endearments of the civilized fair" (McLean in Wallace 1932:284) — to an inland trapping orientation, and this eventually led to the division of the Hamilton Inlet population. Some gravitated to the coast and the cod fishery while others settled inland around the trading posts and oscillated between the summer salmon fishery and winter trapping. The Company became central to the existence of every Settler in the inland region, and trapping became a way of life.

THE ADMINISTRATIVE PERIOD: THE TRANSITION TO A SEDENTARY
LIFESTYLE

The influence of the Depression of the 1920s and 30s was widespread. In Labrador, the loss of fur markets meant that trapping
was no longer a viable way of life. The change in economic orientation, caused by the failing fur trade, was enhanced by several
alternative forms of employment which arose at the beginning of the
twentieth century. The most important of these, from the point of
view of North West River, was the International Grenfell Association
(IGA). However, environmental exploitation, such as mineral exploration, logging, and later, the harnessing of hydro-electric power,
also affected the community and brought about a change from a
seasonally oriented trapping economy to a year-round wage economy. The Second World War, more specifically the construction of
the Airbase at Goose Bay, completed the change which had been
initiated by the Depression. The construction attracted people from
all over Labrador, but most of the employees who stayed for the
duration of the project came from the Settler communities in the
region, and not least from North West River. Thus, North West River
increasingly found itself the focus of various activities, for which it
became the service and administrative centre.

Exploration of the Labrador interior, beginning with the journeys
made by Hudson's Bay Company employees John McLean (1849)
and Erland Erlandson, had been going on for the better part of the
century. North West River became a starting point for many of the
voyages of exploration and adventure into the Labrador 'wilderness.'
One of the earliest expeditions was the 'Eclipse' Expedition which
took place in 1860. The Geological Survey of Canada expedition, led
by Albert Low in 1893–94, was the first scientific survey undertaken
of Labrador, and was an important impetus to subsequent mineral
exploration. Low's published report (1896) of the geology of the
Labrador peninsula also gives some information about the Settler
population of North West River, where he spent time while organiz-
ing his journey.

Other expeditions were often of an adventurous rather than
scientific nature, but, nevertheless, served to draw attention to the
prospects that the Labrador interior offered. The most famous are
those connected with Leonidas Hubbard. In 1903, Hubbard's party
of three men from the New York magazine *Outing* set out from North
West River, heading for Ungava Bay. The expedition proved to be
fatal for the leader, partly because the group had not included a local
guide, and became lost. From this point onwards it became common
to employ North West River trappers as guides on expeditions

inland, and this practice proved to be a lucrative alternative to trapping for some men. Hubbard's attempted expedition was successfully completed by his wife Mina, in the summer of 1905. She raced and finished well ahead of her deceased husband's former companion, Dillon Wallace (Hubbard 1908; Wallace 1915). Mina Hubbard's account of her journey supplied greater knowledge of the terrain she travelled through than had previously been available. Other expeditions were to come.[24]

Following Low in the scientific quest were various teams of scientists who travelled inland in search of minerals. Exploration throughout the first half of the twentieth century culminated in 1953 when the British Newfoundland Corporation (Brinco or Brinex) made its headquarters in North West River (Smith 1975). The Settlers who had given up trapping, many of whom had accompanied earlier expeditions, were now employed as prospectors and field guides for reconnaissance work. Prospecting in some ways compensated for the loss of the trapping lifestyle. It had begun while trapping was still the predominant way of life and it built upon the bush skills and knowledge that the Settlers had acquired as trappers. Furthermore it was seasonal, as opposed to the types of employment that also appeared with the operations of the International Grenfell Association in North West River, and with the construction of the Goose Bay Airbase nearby. This seasonality gave the Settlers some time in which to trap and hunt. As working for the various surveys occurred during the summer months, many prospectors were able to carry on some winter trapping. It was not sufficient, however, to stop the inexorable change in employment pattern from seasonal to year-round wage economy.

After the initial prospecting much of the inland resource development, with the exception of Churchill Falls, occurred without significant effect on the Central Labrador population. Few people moved to western Labrador in search of work; there most of the employees are from the island of Newfoundland. The Churchill Falls project, however, flooded a region more than half the size of Lake Ontario and destroyed a vast hunting and trapping area. The Indians and Settlers who lost traplines, hunting territories and equipment still have bitter memories of this development, and many are loath to trust further development in Labrador. Little good came to Labrador from this hydro-electric project since virtually the entire seven million horsepower output is controlled by Hydro Quebec, which pays less than cost price to Newfoundland.

The Goose Bay Airbase, built during the latter part of the Second World War (in 1941), brought air transportation and direct communication with the outside world to Labrador in the space of a few months. The impact of this was far-reaching, and the transition from one economy to another was not always smooth and painless for the inhabitants of Central Labrador. North West River Settlers remember the transition from trapping to wage labour vividly. The decline in trapping had left the Settlers in desperate need of economic security, and an alternative source of income was essential. While prospecting employed some of the men for some of the time, developments like the Airbase offered reliable full-time employment for a large number of people. The transition, then, was both welcomed and regretted. However, except for causing the relocation of part of the Settler population, work on the Airbase and other forms of construction and maintenance based in Happy Valley-Goose Bay have not been as significant in the development of North West River social structure as has the growth and decline of the International Grenfell Association.[25]

Begun by a visit paid to the Labrador fishery in 1891 by Francis J. Hopwood, a member of the British Board of Trade and of the Council of the Royal National Mission to Deep Sea Fishermen, the International Grenfell Association grew to dominate the life of Central Labrador for the next eighty years. Wilfred Grenfell, experienced and successful with the deep sea fishermen who trawled the North Sea, was given the task of surveying the need for medical and spiritual services among the fishermen who visited Labrador in the summer. In 1892, he visited in the capacity of a Royal National Mission doctor, treating 900 people in that season. Returning to England via St. John's, Grenfell met with various St. John's businessmen and merchants who promised support and encouraged him to come back the next year in order to continue with his work.

Two hospitals were built in Labrador during the following two years, with money raised from St. John's companies. The first of these was built in 1893 at Battle Harbour and the second hospital was built at Indian Harbour in 1894. It can be seen from the location of these premises, and the mandate of the parent organization, that the International Grenfell Association was primarily concerned with the welfare of the 'floater' population (seasonal fishermen). The Indians remained inland and nomadic, the Inuit were charges of the Moravians to the north, and the trapping population only seasonally visited the coast. The Mission's dealings with the inland and native populations did not come until later. The English doctor Harry Paddon, perceiving the need for year-round hospital and medical service to supplement the limited capacity of the two summer stations, moved inland from Indian Harbour during the winter to make use of a facility provided in Mud Lake. In 1916, the small hospital at Mud Lake was moved to a cottage hospital which had been built in North West River.

The International Grenfell Association reflects Grenfell's charismatic personality in its structure and recruiting patterns. "If an order in the way Grenfell perceived his Labrador Mission may be inferred from his actions, he was first an evangelical socialist. ... " (Kennedy 1985:13). Grenfell did not, however, describe his calling to Labrador as at all altruistic:

> Some of my older friends have thought that my decision to go [to Labrador] was made under strong religious excitement, and in response to some deep-seated conviction that material sacrifices or physical discomforts commended one to God. I must, however, disclaim all such lofty motives. I have always believed that the Good Samaritan went across the road to the wounded man just because he wanted to. I do not believe that he felt any sacrifice or fear in the matter. If he did, I know very well that I did not. On the contrary, there is everything about such a venture to attract my type of mind, and making preparations for the long voyage was an unmitigated delight (Grenfell 1919:114).

But he also had decisive ideas about the profession he had chosen. "It is not given to every member of our profession to enjoy the knowledge that he alone stands between the helpless and suffering, and death" (Grenfell 1919:122).

Grenfell had a compassion and admiration for his charges which did not disguise a paternalistic outlook, describing them as both "the Vikings of today," and "merry little people" who:

> Whilst a resourceful and kindly, hardy and hospitable people ... [they] are a reactionary people in matters of religion and education... Christians of a devout and simple faith. The superstitions still found among them are attributable to the remoteness of the country from the current of the world's thought. ... (Grenfell 1932: 142).

For nearly seventy years the International Grenfell Association maintained its strong influence over the lives of the Settlers.

Although the Royal National Mission to Deep Sea Fishermen tried to maintain control of its fledgling mission in Labrador, the IGA increasingly came under the sole jurisdiction of Grenfell. Finally, after several altercations with his superiors, Grenfell left his position in the Royal National Mission in order to devote his undivided attention to the Mission in Labrador. He gradually spent less time as a doctor and spiritual guide in Labrador and concentrated more on touring in America, Canada and Britain, coaxing the money needed to run the Mission from sympathetic audiences of wealthy upper-class people. "Hospitals," Grenfell once said, "are best run, we believe, everywhere, not by government departments, but by philanthropic bodies" (1902:119).

The sons and daughters of this wealthy class also provided a steady stream of volunteers who appeared at the IGA stations during the summer. Helping the Grenfell Mission in Labrador soon became an adventure sought by numerous medical students and volunteers from America and Britain. Although they often worked hard, and to good effect, this transient population created rifts in the social structures of the communities where they stayed. The staff and summer volunteers of the International Grenfell Association added significantly to the outsider and elite subcultures which were developing in North West River. Their inability to fit into the community is seen in the following extract from Kennedy on the hosting of social evenings:

> At such social evenings, Grenfell staff advertized that they would be 'at home' and welcome local guests. Visiting Nurse Anna Jones' description of one such evening at Battle Harbour illustrates the cultural distance between the affluent, educated and probably boisterous Grenfell staff and the shy and subdued local population. Jones writes: "We found the people had no idea of 'taking part' in any games. The first half of the evening was spent by the staff's strenuous and solitary participation in games, such as 'Going to Jerusalem,' and 'Throw the Towel,' to the silent and solemn astonishment of the audience. After considerable urging and actual shoving and pulling a small group were persuaded to take part; and to our joy, and probably for the first time in their lives, lost themselves completely with hilarious laughter in the game."

> Appreciating the diffidence and timidity still characteristic of the local people, I suspect the 'hilarious laughter' Jones triumphantly witnessed was prompted as much by the nervous tension and social ambiguities of such a staged spectacle as by the games themselves. ... These accounts provide some insight into the essentially colonial character of the Grenfell venture, the well-intentioned though patronizing perspective of Grenfell staff and the ability of Settlers to accommodate each summer's influx of these educated, energetic yet impatient representatives of Gesellschaft (1985:21–22).

The IGA was also responsible for an influx of professionals whose advanced education and training, and status as administrators, kept them in a position of superiority in the social structure of the community. Descendants of one of the first administrators of the

North West River hospital, who came from Newfoundland, are still employed as administrative staff today.

Grenfell also frequently gave direct help to the people he came into contact with in Newfoundland and Labrador. One such case was an orphan who earned the title of 'the Mission's own Admirable Crighton and jack of all trades,' and whose descendants were still employed by the International Grenfell Association in 1979. In another instance a family which had fallen on bad times in Nain was moved to North West River by Grenfell, where the father and subsequently several of the sons acquired jobs with the International Grenfell Association. Through such selective patronage, Grenfell and the IGA laid the foundations of what was later to become a locally established elite. We shall explore this matter more fully in Chapters Four and Seven.

Grenfell's involvement in Labrador took him beyond the provision of medical services and 'social guidance' to attempts at improving the living standards of the local population. Several of his schemes for development were successful. He supervised the reintroduction of agriculture (which had declined somewhat after Donald Smith's departure) by creating farms and market gardens. He provided education through boarding schools, and developed and found markets for a local handicraft industry. His attempts to establish co-operatives to lessen the dependence of Settlers upon merchants, to introduce Saami reindeer herders with a herd of reindeer in order to teach animal husbandry to the local population, and to introduce fur farms at Cartwright, were not so successful. Despite the enormous effort involved in implementing many of these operations (both successful and unsuccessful), the Settlers never became more than peripherally involved in the management and control of them. In each case, professionally trained and skilled workers were brought in from outside to manage the experiments and administer the services. The Newfoundland Museum's 1986 exhibition of Grenfell Handicrafts, euphemistically entitled "Helping Ourselves," aptly illustrated the "extrinsic and colonial...nature" (Kennedy 1985:2) of Grenfell's philanthropic experiments. The Mission hired artists and craft teachers from outside who then trained local craftspeople and produced designs for them to copy.

The North West River cottage hospital became the IGA's medical centre for northern Labrador, including the indigenous populations who had at first been ignored by the Mission. But the acquisition of the American Forces' Melville Hospital in Goose Bay during the 1970s had alleviated the need for services from the North West River hospital, and a majority of the immigrant Newfoundland population in Happy Valley-Goose Bay now used the Melville Hospital. At the time it closed in 1983, the North West River hospital was run predominantly by outside professionals with Newfoundland and Settler auxiliary staff who served the indigenous patients. The paternalism with which the IGA was administered had percolated down from the professionals who ran the hospital and other facilities, to the staff, and the Settlers had become 'brokers' (Paine 1971) between the Mission's elite and their patient-clients. A large number of North West River inhabitants had become dependent on the hospital and related institutions for the provision of jobs by the time the Mission withdrew from the community. Ninety jobs were lost immediately when the hospital closed, and several more were expected to be lost during the ensuing withdrawal of services from the community.

In its heyday as the base of the International Grenfell Association, North West River was a hive of activity, its numbers swelled with transient clients for the services provided by schools, boarding homes, and hospital. The presence of these temporary inhabitants boosted the local service economy, such as grocery stores and snack bars. At the same time, the social structure that the International Grenfell Association brought with it inadvertently crystallized the rift between outsiders and Settlers along the lines of skilled and unskilled labour.

North West River is again in a state of flux (1983). The transition to a sedentary life style, which spread over the space of a generation, has left the younger members of the community with limited knowledge of the bush environment or bush occupations. The Town Council and the local development corporation (Mokami Development Association)[26] are planning and reviewing suggestions for alternative economic activities in the region.

For much of the period from the trapping era until after the establishment of the military Base in Goose Bay, the Indians continued to pursue an essentially nomadic, hunting way of life. This kept them inland where they remained relatively unaffected by developments in Central and coastal Labrador. However, with their settlement in the early 1960s, development, especially of the now depopulated interior, is increasingly affecting the Indians also. Following the formation of the Native Association of Newfoundland and Labrador in 1974, the indigenous groups in Labrador have made remarkable political progress, and Labrador Indians now have their own political organization, the Naskapi-Montagnais Innu Association (NMIA), through which they are negotiating a land claims settlement with the Federal Government. The Indians of Central Labrador have also seceded from the municipality of North West River, and they formed their own municipal community of Sheshat-shit in 1979.

The growth of political activity among the Indians has pre-cipitated a flurry of self-reflective activities among the local North West River politicians, who are attempting to strengthen Settler, and community, identities. Settler perceptions of Indian/Settler rela-tions have also been affected by the desire to develop a stronger cultural identity. In the ensuing discussion, by juxtaposing the perceptions Settlers have of themselves with the perceptions they have of Indians, I hope to show how Settlers choose to select elements of their past in constructing a unique Settler identity, and also to illustrate how complex that identity has become.

Portfolio One: 1875–1958

Photograph credits:

Photographs 1 and 10 courtesy of Olive Saunders and *Them Days* Photo Archive

Photographs 2, 5 and 6 courtesy of the Medical Library of Yale University and *Them Days* Photo Archive

Photographs 3 and 4 courtesy of Flora Baikie and *Them Days* Photo Archive

Photographs 7 and 11 courtesy of Max McLean and *Them Days* Photo Archive

Photographs 8 and 9 courtesy of Alfreda Blake and *Them Days* Photo Archive

Photograph 12 courtesy of Jean Crane and *Them Days* Photo Archive

Photograph 1: North West River Settlers and Indians on the steps of the Hudson's Bay Company Store, 1939.

Photograph 2: Dr Wilfred Grenfell with Dr Little and the crew on board the hospital ship *Strathcona*, circa 1907.

Photograph 3: Daniel and Lydia (Brooks) Campbell, circa 1875.

Photograph 4: Mersai and Hannah (Brooks), circa 1890.

Photograph 5: A Settler family out berry-picking on the coast, circa 1895.

Photograph 6: A Settler family on board their schooner, circa 1895. Settlers once used schooners to travel between their winter trapping grounds and summer fishing places.

Photograph 7: Up river! Big Rapids on the Naskapi River, circa 1948. Trappers travelled up river by canoe in September to reach their trapping grounds. They hauled with them supplies to last nearly half a year.

Photograph 8: Down river! Trappers coming down the Hamilton River. Furs were hauled back by toboggan or komatik when the trappers returned to their families for Christmas and the New Year. Canoes taken up in the fall were brought out again during a return trip in the spring. Circa 1940.

Photograph 9: Trapper Sid Blake of North West River, circa 1940. Sid's trapping clothes illustrate the culturally mixed heritage of Central Labrador Settlers: a Naskapi embroidered hunting jacket; 'mukluks' of caribou hide cured by North West River Indians and sealskin mitts.

Photograph 10: A sample of the winter's catch. Duffy Hope and Robert Michelin at Traverspine, 1958.

Photograph 11: Big Tilt, Seal Lake, 1948. Main tilts like this one were used to store the winter's supplies and harvest of furs. A trapper returned to his main tilt approximately once a week. During the week, he spent his nights in smaller tilts which were situated a day's walk from each other along the trapline.

Photograph 12: Trappers in North West River, 1935.

Geographical Orientation to the Community   **3**

Initial settlement in Hamilton Inlet was thinly scattered, as the pattern of seasonal subsistence activities required each family to have a number of home bases spread between the coast and the interior. All home bases had to be situated near water, as the major means of transportation was along waterways both in summer and winter. The types of subsistence activity that occupied pioneer Settlers also called for large territories to harvest, and so families based themselves at considerable distances from one another in order to engage in almost exclusive harvesting. This was true for both summer fishing, in which one or two families fished from a summer settlement, such as Smokey in Groswater Bay, and winter trapping, in which traplines led inland from the home base of a family.[1] A favourite site for a home base was a small river mouth, of which there are many along the northern shore of Lake Melville (see Map 2: Dispersed Settlement in the Lake Melville Region).

This sparse distribution limited the opportunity that any family had for social contact with other families. Neighbours, often several miles apart, were the only inhabitants to be sought out for social visits or help. Both genealogical data and the recorded diaries of these early Settlers show the constraint of geographical distribution on the development of social structures. Whereas the diaries describe how the social activities of the early Settlers were often geographically curtailed, genealogical data is evidence of the limiting effect of geographical distribution, and a numerically small population, on the formation of kin groups.

An important social activity was that of visiting, as Lydia Campbell describes in her diary of 1894:

> Since I last wrote in this book I have been what the people calls
> cruising about hear [sic]. I have been visiting some of my friends
> all though [sic] scattered far apart, with my snow-shoes and axe on

Map 2: Dispersed Settlement in the Lake Melville Region

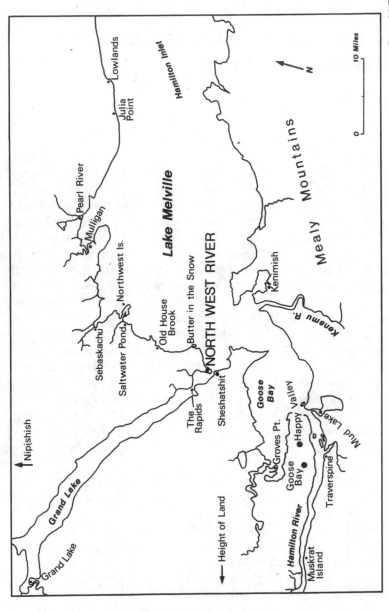

Cartography: Donald Battcock

my shoulders. The nearest house to this place is about five miles up a beautiful river, and then through the woods, what the French calls a portage ... it is what I calls pretty. Many is the time that I have been going with dogs and komatik ... up to North West River to the Hon. Donald A. Smith and family to keep New Year or Easter. ... I have visited last month, on my way up to Sebaskachu, a mountain near by, up to see my dear old sister, Hannah Meshlin, ... My husband and me went up to see him [Hannah's husband], or them. Was not they glad to see the oldest couple in the bay besides themselves. We driving with two dogs and komatik, that was ten miles from them (Campbell 1980:14–15).

Settlers showed great hospitality to those who visited on their way around the bay, and visiting in itself was treated as a festive event. The time expenditure that visiting entailed both made it a valued activity and limited the number of people to whom visits could easily be paid. The term 'cruising' is still in use today to describe a loosely structured form of visiting. It refers to visits paid by groups of family members to the homes of other families. Several such visits are carried out consecutively, with some form of refreshment given at most stops. 'Cruising' has both festive and more regular aspects to it; the regular sort being most frequently done on Sundays. Since subsistence work and commerce were religiously prohibited on that day, Sunday afternoons were fairly regularly spent visiting neighbours around the bays in any particular locality. The dispersed members of family groups, divided up through marriage and the need to space themselves at a distance for fur and fish harvesting purposes, often gathered at their parental home on Sundays as well as on specific festive celebrations.

There were also occasions when the widely dispersed Settlers could meet in larger groups. Settlers often encountered one another in their movements when the change from one type of seasonal activity to another involved moving between bases, as they were usually travelling in the same direction. At such times it was possible to arrange to travel in the company of other Settlers. Moving from the coastal region to the interior or vice versa would involve trading the season's catch, and, with the establishment of the Hudson's Bay Company post at North West River, seasonal visits to the post to sell and buy goods provided the opportunity for get-togethers. The staff and factor of the Hudson's Bay Company often planned to entertain Settlers on certain seasonal occasions such as Christmas and New Year, or the end of the trapping or fishing seasons. Except for these seasonal occasions for socializing, most Settlers were restricted primarily to small family-oriented get-togethers in their visiting.

Early genealogical data (family trees, birth and marriage records) show that geographical location frequently circumscribed the formation of kin relationships. The pattern of inheritance customarily practised by the Settlers in Labrador was ultimogeniture, in which the youngest son, who was usually the last son to remain at home, became the heir and was expected to look after his aging parents when he inherited the home, traplines and fishing berths. This practice meant that at least a part of the same family had been associated with a particular location over many generations, but that each family had also divided and moved to new locations with each generation, thus forming a pattern of family links and extensions along the lake shore. Eligible marriage partners were limited to a small, scattered population, where movement was constrained by time, distance and a rugged environment, and so liaisons between neighbouring families often developed into kin-based social groups. The association of particular families with specific locations is recorded in the many small graveyards scattered along the shore of Lake Melville in which there is a preponderance of one or two family names. Today many Settlers keep a cabin at the site of their family's original home where they frequently spend their free time hunting, trapping and fishing.

Increased development in the region, which culminated with the arrival of the Airbase at Goose Bay, gradually brought about centralization. When settlement in the Lake Melville region became centralized, the social patterns which had developed earlier were, to some extent, transplanted into the community of North West River. These early social and kin-based groups are even now relevant in the social structuring of the community.

The town of North West River is built on a series of sand spits, formed by glacial moraines which divide Lake Melville from Grand Lake and the inland river system of the Naskapi, Susan and Beaver rivers. Each moraine is breached by the river which gave its name to the settlement of North West River.[2] The first breach forms the 'Rapids' at the beginning of Little Lake, and the second breach causes a constriction in the river, called the 'Narrows,' where the town of North West River is situated.

North West River gradually became a settlement as families moved there to make better use of the facilities afforded by the Hudson's Bay Company post, and more recently, by the International Grenfell Association. The Hudson's Bay Company post at Rigolet (the Settler community to the east) and Dickie's Lumber Company at Mud Lake (the Settler community to the south) had also attracted families from around the Inlet. Most people, however, moved from

Map 3: Residential Areas in North West River.

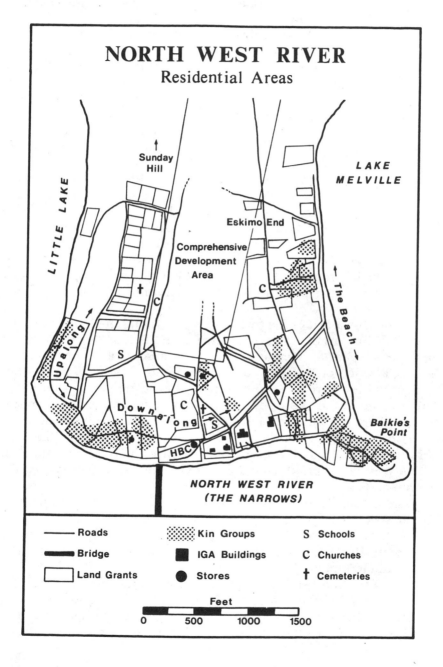

NORTH WEST RIVER
Residential Areas

Sunday
Hill

LITTLE LAKE

LAKE
MELVILLE

Eskimo End

Comprehensive
Development
Area

C

The Beach

Upalong

†

C

S

Down
along

C

†

S

Baikie's
Point

HBC

NORTH WEST RIVER
(THE NARROWS)

—— Roads	▨ Kin Groups	S Schools
▬ Bridge	■ IGA Buildings	C Churches
▭ Land Grants	● Stores	† Cemeteries

Feet

0   500   1000   1500

Cartography: Donald Battcock.

their isolated homes to find work when Goose Bay Airbase was constructed. Each of these phases of development, besides causing centralization, also attracted newcomers.

The town of North West River is divided into a series of sections (see Map 3: Residential Areas in North West River) which, to some extent, mirror the earlier distribution of the inhabitants along the shores of Hamilton Inlet. As water was still the focus of the Settlers' predominantly subsistence economy, and formed the main means of travel throughout the year, early settlement in North West River occurred along the shoreline. The Hudson's Bay Company built its post at the Narrows and from this point the town is divided into 'Upalong,' which is the part of the shore going upstream from the post, and 'Downalong,' which is the part of the shore going downstream from the post. Downalong is a term used to differentiate the rest of the town from Upalong, but is itself divided into a number of sections. The 'Beach,' the 'Eskimo End,' and 'Baikie's Point' are all considered to be part of Downalong. In addition, the term 'Downalong' also refers more specifically to the stretch of road (or river bank) which runs directly behind the Hudson's Bay Company buildings, between the point where the bridge has been constructed and 'Baikie's Point.'

The eastern end of the town faces east along the length of Lake Melville. This part of the town, known as the 'Beach,' is an extension of the Lake Melville shore and terminates at a point in the sand spit called 'Powderhouse Point,' or more recently, 'Baikie's Point,' because that is where most members of the Baikie family live. Along this stretch of the shore there are Settlers who once lived around the northern edge of Lake Melville, between the present site of North West River and the town of Rigolet. The Groves, Campbells, Chaulks, Whites and Baikies all lived at river mouths such as Sebaskashu, North West Islands, Mulligan, Pearl River, and at a small cove called Lowlands (see Map 2).

The Eskimo End of town was built in 1959 to house four Inuit families who were being resettled from Hebron, Nutak and Sagalek in the north. It lies behind the Beach, and terminates at a small Moravian church building, which was originally erected to serve the new inhabitants.

Along the south-facing edge of the sand spit, between Baikie's Point and the Narrows, there are families who had originally settled on the southern shore of Lake Melville at places like Kenimish and Kenamu where they ran the salmon fishery for the Hudson's Bay Company.

Upstream from the Hudson's Bay Company post there are families who had once trapped from points along the Hamilton River or on one of the Grand Lake rivers. Of these families, the Blakes and the Montagues had lived in houses on either side of the Rapids, and the Michelin family had trapped from Traverspine, on the Hamilton River system (see Maps 2 and 3).

The centre of the town grew around the site of the old Hudson's Bay Company post. This is where the new Company store is built, the old post buildings being maintained for storage and warehousing. The store manager lives on an adjacent plot of land. The International Grenfell Association acquired land next to the Hudson's Bay Company area for its hospital. Extensions were periodically added to the original hospital structure, and new facilities were built on the plot of land that was used by the Association. The Mission's facilities, including children's homes and housing for hospital staff, took up a large area in the centre of the town. Now, since the closure of the hospital in 1983, these buildings are gradually coming under the jurisdiction of the town council for community use.

Land grants were issued to private individuals in 1950 by the Department of Crown Lands, after the Airbase was built at Happy Valley-Goose Bay. Land was granted to Settlers who were already occupying it. These early grants were sizeable enough to subdivide when the children of the occupants formed independent households. The sons and daughters of the original owner were often given a section of the land to use for building a house. In other cases, families who were linked through marriage often shared land. All the land around the shore edge was taken early in this period, and since then has swapped hands only through kin groups. In this way, the original land grants were broken up into smaller holdings, and the social group living on each land grant was kin-based (see Map 3, p. 47).

In sum, the dispersed settlement pattern is repeated on several levels in the community of North West River. Not only do the sections of town mirror an earlier geographical distribution, but within each section, the already established kin-based groups are perpetuated. To begin with, families moved from scattered settlements to particular areas of the town, so that the sections of the town roughly correspond to an earlier scattered settlement pattern. Families who were neighbours when they lived along the shores of Hamilton Inlet are still neighbours in town. This linkage has been reinforced through preferential marriage. Each section of town, then, is inhabited by families from the same part of the Inlet. The sections in town represent kin-based groups, and the subdivision of land grants

amongst family members subsequent to their settlement has perpetuated this pattern.

The physical dimensions of the town have helped to perpetuate
a segregation between the sections. A plan of the town (see Map 3)
shows that each section roughly follows a pathway which radiates
from the central area, in which the store, clinic and bridge are
situated. In the normal course of events there is little reason to go
from one part of town to another unless it is specifically to visit
friends. The various sections of town resemble street communities.
A member of one such community may not know the place of
residence of someone from another part of town, or be aware of
housing developments at the other end of town. Friends may be
visited in other parts of town, but, for various reasons which will be
explored later, friendships have always had a tendency to develop
in relation to already established kinship and geographical patterns.
Since the families of friends usually lived in the same part of town
as the friends, there had, until recently, seldom been reason to visit
other parts. The geographical and social division is particularly
marked with regard to Upalong and Downalong where there have
been few kinship links established between community members
living in these two sections of town since its settlement. It has often
been the case that those who marry out of one area into another
have, to a large degree, lost close contact with the kin they have left
behind.

Newcomers are a recurrent feature of Hamilton Inlet life; they
have arrived (and are still arriving) at specific times to fill specific
needs in the community as required. We have seen that the
Hudson's Bay Company brought Orcadians to the area during the
fur trade, many of whom stayed on after their contracts were
completed. The International Grenfell Association employed most of
its professional staff from outside the community, and although
many of these specialists were only temporary residents, a number
of families and individuals have stayed in the community. IGA
employees were often given housing on part of the Association's land
grant, and so have become members of a town centre subcom-
munity.

However, because of population pressures, these patterns are
being disrupted, and contemporary North West River residents are
seeing many changes in the community's traditional social and
geographical patterns. The original land grants are now fully occupied and children born in the third generation after these land
grants were made are forced to look elsewhere for land on which to
build their homes. Land close to the rest of the family is sought

whenever possible, but this is increasingly difficult to find. Now grants to Crown Lands are made through the town council which is preparing new areas to meet the request for land grants. The new development areas are removed from the shoreline and the size of a grant is suitable for one house only. The need for building lots has ruptured the kin-based pattern of the town's geography. These areas are not geographical extensions of the areas already in existence, and so far, have not become extensions of kin groups either. Identification with particular sub-groups in the community has weakened with the move inshore. In relation to the kin-based sub-communities that had developed previously, the new residential areas are becoming 'no man's lands.'

Some of the buildings erected by the International Grenfell Association are now used to house community offices and a clinic, but others are unoccupied. The Hudson's Bay Company retains and uses the original post buildings, the store building and a house on a plot of land for the store manager and family. Brinco, the mineral exploration company, withdrew its activities from the community concurrently with the International Grenfell Association, and it has also left buildings unoccupied in the town. The construction, in 1979, of the bridge, which crosses the river and enters town just to the west of the Hudson's Bay Company area, has curtailed the activities which were once associated with more co-operative methods of crossing the river (to be discussed further in Chapter Six). The slackening pace has meant that there is a quietness owing to inactivity in this once busy central area.

Recently the town council upgraded the community's roads — from snowmobile paths to wider gravelled roads — in order to keep up with the development of the paved road to Goose Bay and the bridge which gives outside vehicles access to the community. In connection with the upgrading, all the community's roads and paths were named and signposted. Whereas, before, each section of the town was known by a local name such as Downalong, gradually these terms are falling into disuse while the use of road names is becoming increasingly common. At the same time the town is spreading into newly developed residential areas which cannot be categorized as belonging either to Upalong or to Downalong. This difficulty with categorizing springs as much from the nature of the social groups that occupy the new areas as it does from a geographical problem. What is clear, however, is that the earlier pattern of social networks is gradually being eroded.

Kith and Kin   4

The Analysis of Kinship Patterns in
North West River and their Effect on the
Formation of the Oldtimer-Newcomer-Outsider
Social Character Continuum

In the ensuing discussion, genealogical data is used to explore the
formation of kin-groups in the community: data which has been
gathered from individuals in North West River, Bibles and other
privately owned documents as well as from church and archival
records. The genealogical data given here relate back to the early
history of Central Labrador settlement, and this discussion builds
upon information set out in the first section of Chapter Two. The
discussion considers the importance of the pioneer period in the
perceptions of present-day Settlers, then turns to the development
of the 'oldtimer'[1] social character, and allows for its consideration
in relation to the social characters of 'newcomer' and 'outsider.'

The social character of 'oldtimer' resides in the ability to trace
descent to the first pioneer Settlers to arrive in Hamilton Inlet, and
is used by all members of long-established families, regardless of
age. The claim of descent from one of the pioneer families has two
implications for Settler identity. Firstly, the original European Settlers in Hamilton Inlet married Inuit, so to claim descent through
these families implies native status. Secondly, the original Settlers
represent the beginning of European settlement history in the
region, so the claim of descent is also a claim to superior historical
association with the region. The political use of superior historical
association with the region is similar to the political use of 'occupation since time immemorial' used by indigenous populations in the
process of claiming land from the Federal and Provincial Governments. The claim is that a group's right to exercise rights and
privileges in an area grows proportionally with the length of time
that group can claim to have been associated with the area. In legal
terms, however, aboriginality is given precedence. But in the eyes of
the Settlers, the concept of 'oldtimer,' with its relationship to Inuit

and European pioneer ancestry, is similar to the concept of aboriginality.

Although there were several pioneer Settlers in Hamilton Inlet, most oldtimer families recognize common ancestry through an Englishman named Ambrose Brooks or, more specifically, one of his daughters—Lydia. This recognition can be attributed to the fact that Lydia, who became Lydia Campbell by her second marriage, kept a diary of her life with her family during the early years of settlement in Hamilton Inlet. Publication of the diary (in *The Evening Herald*, 1894 and reproduced by *Them Days*, 1980) has made knowledge of these early years accessible to the community and has focused attention on the part played by Lydia and her family during that period of history. Brooks had three daughters: the eldest, Elizabeth, drowned with her husband and family; Hannah and Lydia survived. Both surviving daughters married twice and produced families with each marriage. Descendants of the two women have formed separate clusters of kin within the larger Brooks-related kin-groups of the community, and these clusters tended to be endogamous. Among other things, the division between the kin of the two daughters is partly responsible for the formation of Upalonger-Downalonger differences in the contemporary community of North West River (see Chapter Seven).

Despite the fact that the absorption of newcomers has always been a facet of the kin-group structure of Hamilton Inlet, the main kin-groups tended initially to be primarily endogamous because of isolation and a limited population. A useful concept in analysing genealogical information collected in North West River is found in Murdock (1949 and 1967) where the term 'deme' is given to a locally endogamous community. Murdock points out that the practice of endogamy is a transitional phase in the case of the deme, and cannot be perpetuated for any length of time because of problems arising from the incest taboo. Murdock's definition of deme does not apply precisely to the situation in North West River because he states that endogamy cannot be considered to be a pattern of kinship if it is the result of the isolation of a group from other groups. However, despite the fact that endogamy began because of isolation, it persisted in Hamilton Inlet when the population was no longer isolated and when the families of Lydia and Hannah had divided. And indeed, marriages between first cousins and other closely related kin were common in the community's past. I have used the term deme, then, to describe the kin-groups which were formed by Lydia and her sister Hannah.

Hannah, born in 1813, was the older of the two. She married William Mesher from Groswater Bay in the 1820s. William's father, William Mesher senior, came out to the Labrador coast from the Channel Islands as a fisherman.[2] He married an Inuk and settled on the coast. The Meshers must have been contemporaries of the Brooks'. William junior and a brother of his, John, are both mentioned as 'planters' in the Hudson's Bay Company journal for North West River (then called Fort Smith) in 1836. Hannah was fifteen when her first child, Robert, was born. Robert married and raised a large family on the coast. Hannah's daughter by her first marriage, Esther, married and settled in Cartwright, but remained childless, as did her second son, Ambrose, who was crippled. The Hudson's Bay Company journal mentions the death of a young boy, Peter Mesher, who may also have been the son of William and Hannah. There is no record of William Mesher's death, but Hannah married again and had three more sons.

Her second husband was a French Canadian called Mersai (or Marcel) Michelin, who came from Trois Rivieres in Quebec in 1834. Descendants of their sons still inhabit North West River. Hannah's son Peter Michelin married Rebecca Blake, the daughter of Lydia's brother-in-law (John Blake), and their descendents either moved away or became absorbed into the Blake family. Her second son, John, married twice. Both daughters of his first marriage became Blakes, but the children of his second marriage remained in what later became the Michelin deme. Joseph, the youngest son, also married twice. Two daughters survived from the first marriage; one married John Montague, an Orkneyman who came to work for the Hudson's Bay Company in 1873, and the other married John's son, Robert Montague. Joseph's second marriage produced several sons, two of whom married Montagues. Michelins and Montagues have intermarried frequently since then, thereby creating the core of the Michelin deme, and descendents of John and Joseph Michelin and John Montague still live in Upalong.

Ambrose Brooks' younger daughter Lydia (born in 1818), married William Blake, the son of another pioneer family, and her descendents belong to the Blake deme. William Blake's father, William senior, arrived as a fisherman with the Slade Company, and while very little is known about him, he may have come from southern Devonshire, where the name Blake is common. In an affidavit for the Labrador Boundary Dispute,[3] William's grandson claims that the Blake family had been in Hamilton Inlet for 140 years. The claim was made in 1910, which would date William senior's arrival on the coast at around 1770. It is more likely that he arrived during the 1780s, since Slade's were not active in the region before that date.[4] William Blake senior had other children besides William: John, who married and settled in Rigolet, and George[5] and Esther, (who may have been husband and wife rather than siblings). William and his brother, John, are both mentioned in the 1836 North West River Hudson's Bay journal as 'planters.' The Blake family Bible records that John married Sarah, and that they had nine children between the years 1832 and 1857. Their daughter Rebecca married Hannah's son Peter. The origins of John Blake's wife, Sarah, are unknown, but Lydia mentions three sisters-in-law and a mother-in-law in her diary, and so they must have been living in the 1830s.

Lydia and William junior had several children, but only two survived to adulthood: Susan and Thomas. Susan married a Captain Irving and moved to Sept Iles, where she died, leaving her husband and one son. Thomas lived to the age of 95 and became a renowned figure in the Inlet, marrying four times. These four marriages produced only four surviving children, however, and it seems that a majority of the Blakes still living in Hamilton Inlet must be the descendents of John, William's brother.

Lydia is called 'widow Blake' in the 1845 Hudson's Bay Company journal, by which time she had already remarried. Her second husband, Daniel Campbell, was the cooper for the Company who had come out to North West River from Orkney in the 1840s. Their daughter, Margaret, also married a Company worker called Thomas Baikie, who came from a once-wealthy Orkney merchant family.[6] Of the Campbells' five sons, John and Alexander survived to adulthood; both married and settled on the coast in order to pursue the fishery. Most of the Campbells in Labrador today are in Cartwright and vicinity. Descendants of John and William Blake, Lydia and her daughter, Margaret Baikie, form the Blake deme, who live in Downalong, Baikie's Point and the Beach areas of North West River.

The family names of Blake, Baikie, Michelin and Montague have gained attention because of their preponderance among other names in the community, because of their occurrence in Lydia Campbell's diary, and because of the tendency of the descendents to have settled in North West River rather than another community. These are not, however, the only names which confer oldtimer status in North West River. Family names such as Best, Groves, Oliver, Shephard and Rumbolt also confer the status of oldtimer, but although they still exist in other Labrador communities, they have largely been lost through marriage in North West River.

From the experiences of oldtimers and oldtimer families, traits are drawn upon to create the 'oldtimer' social character. This social character has developed in opposition to others which have evolved out of the experiences of the community's newcomers and outsiders. In the following discussion the experiences of newcomers and outsiders are contrasted with those of the oldtimer families, thus also tracing the development of 'newcomer' and 'outsider' social characters. Quotation marks are used to distinguish social characters from people in the ensuing discussion.

The pioneer families of the West Country fishermen and their Inuit wives form the historical first layer of the heterogeneous North West River population, from which the social character of 'oldtimer' arises. Oldtimers (and old trappers) form the mainstream of North West River society, and are acknowledged by other community members as having a familiarity with the customs of Labrador life. For example, putative knowledge of kinship networks and the changes which have shaped the development of the community are part of the 'oldtimer' social character. The 'oldtimer' social character, then, is vested with the affiliations of an extensive kinship network, and interests in and ties to Labrador as a homeland and place of origin. Both of these characteristics apply decreasingly to the experiences of newcomers and outsiders. The 'oldtimer' character is placed in contrast to the characters of 'newcomer' and 'outsider,' which are also formed from the experiences of community members. In the discussion below, we shall explore the distinctions between newcomers and outsiders in the community, and how traits from the experiences of both newcomers and outsiders have been used in the formation of these social characters.

People arriving in the community are seen by other community members as being either newcomers or outsiders, and the distinction depends upon the situation and origin of the new arrival. While the social characters of both 'newcomer' and 'outsider' can be placed in opposition to the 'oldtimer' social character, both 'newcomer' and 'outsider' have distinguishing characteristics. Newcomers are people who have moved permanently to the community but are not members of the oldtimer families. Outsiders are those who are sojourning in the community for employment reasons, and constitute a number of professionals (e.g. teachers and nurses) who intend to move on after gaining adventure, and experience or variety in their work.

The line between newcomer and outsider blurs when either marries into the community and, in some cases, becomes part of an oldtimer family. Such marriage in itself does not endow the individual with oldtimer status, and the traits pertaining to the social characters of 'newcomer' and 'outsider' do not fade. Thus, an individual who arrived as an outsider, and who then married into the community—thus becoming a newcomer, can retain the traits and perceptions which mark the 'outsider' social character—therefore espousing the social character of 'outsider.'

Like the 'oldtimer' social character, which can be espoused by the young and old members of oldtimer families alike, the social characters of 'outsider' and 'newcomer' can be espoused by Settlers who are not new to the community, or are not considered to be newcomers or outsiders by other community members. The occasions upon which the social characters of 'oldtimer,' 'newcomer' and 'outsider' can be espoused by Settlers who have not had the relevant experiences are limited both by the social situation and by the other participants in the social interaction. For instance, oldtimers can make jokes about Indians like newcomers, as long as the perceptions implied by the jokes are later qualified by the Settlers when they resume their own character with different perceptions of Indians. The social character of 'outsider' can likewise be espoused by other Settlers in certain social situations.

Newfoundlanders joined English and Scottish newcomers in forming separate sub-groups in the community's past, beginning with the first major influx attracted by the Hudson's Bay Company. These sub-groups have become associated with the different sets of traits and perceptions which form the social characters of 'newcomer' and 'outsider.' As we have seen, the fundamentally class-based social structure of the Hudson's Bay Company created an early elite of outsiders who sojourned in Labrador as well as introducing newcomers who married and remained permanently in the region. The family names that date back to the influx of Hudson's Bay Company workers from Orkney are considered to have oldtimer status for several reasons. More often than not these Orkneymen married into the pioneer families already settled in the region, and eventually they outnumbered the original pioneers. Their influx, in conjunction with the economic influence of the Hudson's Bay Company, caused a significant change in the economic and social structure of the community which has since helped to shape and colour Settler identity. However, the Hudson's Bay Company officers who sojourned in North West River retained the status of outsiders, and continued to form an elite.

More recently, the International Grenfell Association caused people to migrate to North West River. Many of the Mission's professional workers were drawn from Britain (particularly England, but also mainland Scotland). Most of these workers sojourned in Labrador, and were instrumental in bringing about further economic and social change in the community. Sojourning professionals were rarely considered anything but outsiders to the community, since they usually arrived as family units or married outside the community, sent their children away to schools, and eventually returned to their countries of origin. These International Grenfell Association professionals associated with, and gradually absorbed the old Hudson's Bay Company elite, who were also of English and mainland Scottish origin.

At present 'elite' is not a term used by North West River Settlers — there is no such term used in the community — but a group of families is recognized and renowned for their influential position in North West River local affairs. These families are those who were directly related to or helped by the older Hudson's Bay Company and IGA elites. Today, several members of these families fill positions in local level politics such as town councillors and other government workers.

Increasingly, trained workers were drawn from sources closer to North West River. These newcomers seldom joined the English-related elite. Nursing and teaching staff moved from other Newfoundland and Labrador communities which were engaged in International Grenfell Association operations, and some married into the North West River community. People who are relatively new to the community, but who have come to stay have frequently formed into sub-communities of newcomers, which are based upon place of origin. Newfoundlanders are a case in point.

The International Grenfell Association introduced many Newfoundlanders to the community during the last few decades, and there are Newfoundland family names which span one or two generations in North West River, but they have not yet achieved full oldtimer status. Their arrival in the community has been incremental rather than overwhelming, and so they have not had the social and economic effect that the influx of Hudson's Bay Company workers had.

Recently incorporated Newfoundlanders still form a separate social group in North West River, as my experience of Christmas jannying illustrates.[7] I was invited to go jannying by three Newfoundland women, two of whom had originally come to North West River as nurses from the hospital in St. Anthony, and had since married into the community. Jannying, or mummering, involves visiting friends while dressed up in costumes which disguise identity. Jannies are traditionally offered refreshment by those they visit.

It is seen by Newfoundlanders as a Newfoundland custom. One of the women explained that they (the St. Anthony women) had often wanted to go jannying before, but had not because they felt that there were few people in North West River who would understand. In the present context, however, jannying was also used to reinforce group feelings between the various Newfoundland women who had married into the community.

We began the evening by planning a route around the community which would allow visits to be paid to as many friends of the three participants as possible. Visits were suggested and either added to the itinerary or vetoed, according to the expected response of the visitees. Typical comments were: "Sure no, girl! They wouldn't know what to do with a bunch of Jannies!" or; "Now, they'll invite us right along in!" Hence, nearly all the visits we made as jannies that evening were to the houses of Newfoundlanders and the expedition proved that Newfoundlanders form a distinct group in the community in both their own eyes and those of the community.

The pockets of newcomers in the community, such as are formed by the Newfoundland group, and the oldtimer community members, are distinguished from each other by their social characters, which are based on the different historical and cultural experiences of each group. The social character of 'oldtimer' provides Settlers with elements of social and ethnic identity which are based upon the two claims of historical superiority (long-term residence), and of native status through Inuit ancestry. Since the social character of 'oldtimer' is based upon the claim to long-term residence in, and familiarity with, Labrador, then 'oldtimers' can also claim to have a familiarity with Indian culture, which has been gained through the past experiences of trappers. None of these experiences, which are crucial elements in Settler identity, are shared by newcomers to the community. This has the effect of separating newcomers, and the social character based upon the experiences of the newcomer, from the mainstream of North West River society.

The experiences of newcomers separate them from mainstream North West River society in several ways. Firstly, in not having Inuit ancestry, newcomers forego the claims to native status made by oldtimer Settlers. Other social characters are espoused to enable them to express security in, and affinity with, their environment. Secondly, newcomers perceive Indians as unconflictually separate from their own cultural identity; hence, the perceptions they express about Indians are much more open in their prejudices and lack of familiarity.

A conversation I held with a Newfoundland shopkeeper in the community illustrates this point. The woman had been a workmate of mine during a previous stay, and I often went into her shop both to talk and to purchase goods. During one such visit I asked her whether many Indian customers used her shop, and she replied that she saw a few. She went on to explain that she did not trust them, although, apparently, they had not given any cause for this mistrust. She also explained that Indians would never do as assistants in the shop because they were not reliable. I asked her why she thought that they would be untrustworthy, and she replied by reminding me of an Indian acquaintance with whom we had previously worked:

> Sure girl, you remember Mary-Jane? She never showed up for work. Out of the three months that she worked for us, she was there for about three weeks!

Other negative responses, such as "Indians don't deserve special status or special rights," "they bring their problems upon themselves," "they're lazy and deceitful," and "there are people, and then there's *Indians*," were also most usually made by newcomers. When oldtimer Settlers spoke negatively about Indians they prefaced or qualified their statements with positive remarks. This is because their perceptions of Indian/Settler relations, unlike those of newcomers, are compromised by references to shared Indian or Inuit cultural traits.

The social character of 'newcomer,' then, is constructed by juxtaposing the experiences of newcomers with those of oldtimers, as is outlined above. As a result of their lack of affiliation with the land and region and their lack of association with native cultures and ancestry, the social characters of 'newcomer' and 'outsider' reject Indian cultural traits and Inuit ancestry. In social interactions, this rejection of Indian and Inuit cultural components of Settler identity often puts them in conflict with the 'oldtimers.' This is the primary basis on which 'oldtimers' stand in contrast to 'newcomers.'

A further extension of this dichotomy is given by the social character of the 'outsider.' In order to examine the development of the 'outsider' social character, and its juxtaposition with 'oldtimer' and 'newcomer,' I shall draw upon an early experience in my fieldwork. Before moving into North West River, I spent a day wandering around in the community in search of lodgings. Rita was one of the first inhabitants I met, and she and her husband offered to take me round the community to look for lodgings. Rita directed us from one home to the next, and the occupants of the homes she selected shared several traits. The people she selected were usually the professional staff of the International Grenfell Association and other institutions. They were living alone in houses with amenities such as spare bedrooms, central heating systems, televisions and electric stoves. None of the people she selected were from North West River, or elsewhere in Labrador, but had come from either Britain, mainland Canada or America. Rita had, in fact, taken us to the homes of outsiders. She had two reasons for selecting the homes of these people out of other possible lodgings in the town. Firstly, she explained that they lived alone and so might welcome someone else to live with them. They also had room to spare for another occupant, a luxury not shared by many of the Settler families. Secondly, she had classified me as part of this group, and felt that I would have more in common with a fellow outsider than I would with a local resident.

The category of outsider is well illustrated by this example. Outsiders, like newcomers, do not rely upon tenuous links with indigenous cultures in maintaining and manipulating social identity. They constitute a group of people attracted to the community for reasons of work, but who do not intend to stay for more than a few years. This means that they bring with them a style of living which is alien to the rest of the community and, in maintaining this style of living in the face of considerable odds, they form a ghetto within the community.[8]

Traits which mark the 'outsider' social character include elements from the lifestyle maintained by visiting professionals. One of these traits is an interest in collecting various artifacts produced in the north. Artifacts collected in North West River include rare old books on various expeditions undertaken by European and American explorers during the nineteenth century. A vicarious interest (in the case of outsiders) in the history of the region has developed in conjunction with the interest in rare old books about Labrador.

Outsiders frequently act as patrons to both Indians and Settlers. This is because, through their work—mostly as professionals—they occupy relatively prestigious and powerful positions in the community, and they are able to maintain contacts with the outside world. Many outsiders are also active in local politics. The effect of all this is that the local elite is infiltrated, if not constituted, by outsiders. It also means that the traits of the 'outsider' social character are shared with members of the elite and the 'outsider' social character is frequently espoused by the latter in their social interactions. And so, the self-perceptions associated with the 'outsider' social character include those of patron, guardian and local historian.

Both 'outsiders' and 'newcomers,' then, are in contrast with 'oldtimers' for different reasons. Neither shares the cultural and historical experiences that make affiliation with the indigenous population part of their cultural identity, and yet this separation from the mainstream of North West River community life is approached in contrasting ways by outsiders and newcomers. In sum, the traits which symbolize the 'newcomer' social character, and separate it from the social character of the 'outsider,' are: (1) the distance from *and* (2) the rejection of the Indian and Inuit components of the Settler identity. The traits which separate the 'outsider' social character from mainstream North West River society, and from the social character of 'newcomer,' are: (1) the maintenance of an identity which is divorced from mainstream Settler society, which allows for (2) objective interests in the surrounding but separate cultures, and (3) affiliations with the elite and political groups in the community. Elements of these distinct approaches to North West River community life, and the perceptions which arise from them, come into play as social characters in the juggling of Settler social identity.

Them Days   5

The Significance of a Trapping Past
to the Shaping of Settler Identity
and the Formation of Social Characters
in North West River

Social characters represent nodes in a volatile social environment
which coalesce around perceptions and identities which are themselves grounded in, and extrapolated from, different social experiences. The intention of this chapter is to point out elements in
trappers' descriptions of the trapping way of life which have been
used to symbolize the 'trapper' in contemporary social interaction
in North West River, and, thus, to trace the development of the
'trapper' as a social character.

The social character of 'trapper' has evolved out of the occupational role of the Settlers who trapped with the Hudson's Bay
Company for a living (and who will be referred to as trappers without
the use of quotation marks). As Chapter Two illustrates, the
Hudson's Bay Company was extremely influential in shaping
Central Labrador society during the days of the fur trade. The social
character of 'trapper' makes symbolic use of certain activities associated with trapping. Trapping as the major economic activity
occupied a period in the history of the community recent enough to
shape and colour the memories of many of the community's older
people. It represents an adaptation to the environment which con-
trasts North West River Settlers with the Settlers of other coastal
communities where the major economic activity had become fishing,
and where Inuit maritime harvesting skills had been adopted rather
than the bush skills associated with Indians. North West River
Settler culture is also unique among Canadian Settler cultures
because, as we have seen, trapping had become the domain of the
Central Labrador Settlers not of the Indians as was the case in the
rest of Canada. Thus, the social character of the 'trapper' symbolizes
a unique and colourful past for contemporary Settlers — a fact which

is becoming increasingly apparent to Settlers, and is of great importance to the formation of Settler identity.

The way of life imposed by the fur trade gave trappers a significant social arena away from the community. In the 'bush,'
patterns of social interaction developed which were peculiar to the
lifestyle, and it is upon these patterns that the character of the
'trapper' has been built. 'Trappers'' perceptions of Indians are embedded in a complex matrix of symbols which are used to represent
an adherence to the values of the trapping lifestyle when they are
expressed in contemporary social interactions. An appreciation of
the differences between Indian and Settler bush skills, and the
hospitality, commensality and interdependence between Settlers
and Indians in the bush, are the perceptions which symbolize the
'trapper' social character. However, the 'trapper' social character
carries with it many perceptions about Settler identity other than
those specifically about the Settlers' relationship with Indians.

The descriptions below come from three Settlers whom I inter-
viewed individually about their lives as trappers. They show the
richness of the cultural heritage that the trapping lifestyle affords
North West River Settlers. Elements of the three conversations have
been arranged in order to give as full an account as possible of the
trappers' activities while maintaining both the integrity of the individual contributions and the emphases which the Settlers
themselves place on certain activities and social interactions.

Alfred Dunn,[1] 74, lives in Downalong. He cut his own trapline
along the Drunken River valley in the Mealy Mountains when he was
a young man, during the peak of the fur trade. He spent many years
trapping in that area before turning to prospecting when the Depression made trapping unviable. His contributions give the most
detailed descriptions of the trapper's activities in the country.
Jerome Scarlet is an Upalonger in his late sixties, who trapped for
seventeen years before the Depression forced him to seek another
occupation. George Beech is a Downalonger in his mid-fifties, who
trapped for a few years with his father, and who now works for the
Federal Government Department of Crown Lands. Often a trapper's
first experience of trapping would be on his father's path; later, the
young man may branch off from his father and begin to cut his own
path. This was the case with George. He was a boy of thirteen when
he first set out alone to trap on part of his father's trapline, to the
north of the community.

The descriptions begin with George relating his experiences on
the first trapping journey he made alone. The first trip out alone is
a 'rite of passage'[2] for trappers, and many of those I spoke to showed

pride in stressing their young age and ability to overcome the fear that grows out of isolation during that initial season.

George: [I began trapping] when I was about twelve or thirteen years old. Lonely! First time I went in Nipishish[3] with my father, trapping... starting 25th September, 'n' I came back in January. I was six weeks on my own that time. All by myself, without seeing my father. That's a long time to go. I never got frightened. Lonely, though! Especially if you're laid up in bad weather and that, not doin' nothing—tired.

The Indians was always out in the woods, them days, always in round Nipishish. I'd see them in the winter. [They would] come to your cabin, sometimes in the night time. Not a person around, and all of a sudden, a knock at your door! Heh! Three more Indians. I was in there one time, my first year in there, and I got the biggest fright of my life! In the tilt[4] and not a soul round, then all of a sudden round pulls the tarp 'n' in crawls 'n Indian! Ha ha heh! Stayed an' had a cup of tea, and talked and took off again, that night, to his camp, nine hours away! He'd been hunting, chasing some caribou down across and had come across my track and chased me! He came in for a cup of tea! That feller Selma—he died last year—Philip Selma, a tall feller. He used to be my buddy! He'd visit every year—come across from Snegamook. [He would spend the] summer in that area and he'd always come across. A long way, they'd come. Awful good, them Indians, to help. They'd do anything for you! You'd go across to their tent, camp—where they had their tents and that—and they'd do anything for you. Offer you anything to eat, cup of tea and anything, eh?

Alfred: I trapped over towards the Gulf of St. Lawrence, over that way, see? Well, I'd meet up with the Indians over from the Gulf of St. Lawrence way, Quebec. They used to come over every year. They'd come over to Traverspine and then they'd stay there until about February, I guess. When it got a bit warmer to take the families back, then they moved 'em back—all the way back to the Gulf of St. Lawrence again! They just come to Traverspine, that's all! The men'd come down 'ere, sell their fur, and take their food back to Traverspine. Then they'd haul it all back in the winter—so far, and get back to where they were and trap then, see? Stay there and trap, and hunt the caribou. We wouldn't see Indians until they came up from the Gulf of St. Lawrence. And then, chance time you'd see them. Oh, you would see them at Traverspine—same crowd, over from the Gulf of St. Lawrence. There were a lot of them then. Quite a lot. Some of the men [would visit], but they were just passing through, then, on their way out. They had their families with them, you see. [They would] travel with their families. I s'pose 'twas good for them—the Indians—but then they had to hunt all the time, hunt meat. Try to get meat for the family. That was a lot of work. Trap and get meat! [The women used to] cut wood, clean the meat, make snowshoes—everything like that. Clean the caribou skin. It was hard work for them all. Imagine all them little small children out before daylight! 'Twas cold, you know. They were well dressed, though. They worked in slow, they took their time. With them—with the Indians—wherever they were caught was home. They trapped different from us, you see, they might be one place one year and pass on to another place the next year. But we had our same trapline.[5] All our traps was there.

Jerome: [The Indians] may be trapping and hunting as they go, you see. [They] stay awhile in one place—trapping, and then go on for another old deer or something, and stop, and go on to another place where they want to stop for a while. And then they stay there until they want to move back again, you know. But they used to have hard times. They'd get down pretty low on food—low down on food and hungry and that kind of stuff, you know. When they come out, they wouldn't have nothing left, only their pipe! They'd be chewin' on their pipe! Ah ha!

Alfred: [I used to trap along] Drunken River. They used to pass there a lot. Some Indians used to come out just by where I have to go, just below. Different places, they used to come. Some of them would come from Natashquan. Some more from Musquaro. Some from St. Augustin, Mingan, Seven Islands [Quebec North Shore communities]. All up that way, with the little small children. Little tiny things walking, you know! We'd visit them when we were passing like that … they might be right up on our trapline, eh? We had to pass them, you know, go in their tent, talk with them, have something to eat. Good. Very good. Awful kind!

Good people. Wonderful kind people. If you go to their tents they couldn't do enough for you.

I almost always bought my sled [and snowshoes] from the Indians—the ones from St. Augustin or the ones in Mud Lake. There were a lot of Indians in Mud Lake.[6] That's where I'd buy 'em. They were good to haul, smooth. Some of them [snowshoes] had little small beaver tails, you know. Oh, that was good snowshoes! Light, and they were better to walk. They were really close-knitted—the bear[paw] ones. But those long-tailed ones were no good to us people, not a bit of good. When you're haulin' a sled, you've got to get close to the sled, eh? Right close to it. But with the long-tailed snowshoes you couldn't have 'er close because the nose of the sled would be on top of the snowshoes the whole time. No good, you see? When you're hauling, you trip yourself all the time with that! But the short ones—wide and short—they were the best.

Jerome: They [the Indians] were good old fellers, you know! A lot of fine old fellers and all of that kind of stuff. We always used to help them out in the country. They wanted something from us, and we would give it, as long as we had enough. You can't always, though—you'd have nothing left for yourself, you know. But they was good in the bush and that area. If you needed something and they had it. ... And it would go like that. But, uh! That's the only way you can survive in the country—one man to another, and stuff like that. Even going up in canoe—'e might tip over 'n' you'd lose a lot of your food. I know of some times...we'd give a little bit of this and a little bit of that, everybody'd give a little bit of this and a little bit of that, you know! Then he [the person with the upset canoe] got enough food. You see what I mean, eh?—Well, you know, getting wet. Flour is O.K. It dries out and just gets hard. Then you've got a flour bag like plaster! Inside or outside, it couldn't get any wetter! You could [eat it] if you had to. If you ran out, you'd have to. All you have to do is get some hot water and mix it up and make flour soup! Ha!—And that's the way it works, 'cause a guy could lose every damned thing, eh? Case like that, you might have to come back—give up and start over again. That was the way it worked!

Alfred: 'Twas a wonderful life though, trapping! If I had my life again, I'd do it. We lived on the meat [we caught]. We start eating meat in the fall and we eat meat until we get home! Oh, we couldn't take too much, you know! Used to take flour and baking powder and stuff, you know. Little dried things like raisins, and perhaps sometimes some apricots. Something like that, you know. We ate little of that, though. Few raisins, rice. Rice is good. I mean, rice—you could make a good pot of rice soup, then—takes a very little rice. Up through Kenamu River to Drunken River. We had to portage six miles up the side of a hill, until you get up on the top! You get up on the top, and you get a long slope down to the river. That was good, going down gradually. That was awful good to see, like the battle was over. But it took about five trips. You do it in five trips— that's with four loads of the food, and one with the canoe. Heavy loads, though! All you could take there.

George: Find your way through, blaze a tree every now and then ...that's all! Follow water, more or less. In the end of it you make a path [trapline].

Alfred: Every man had his trapline, and nobody bothered another man's trapline. Oh no! Might take a skin of fur and hang it up there for you, if you're passing. Might see a skin of fur in somebody's trap, you'd hang it up and set the trap again. But you wouldn't go no closer. I mean you wouldn't go no closer to the trap, because, if you did, perhaps the other trapper might not know why you come there, where his trap is. Very particular, you see. That was your trapline. That was the way you had to make money. That was it. No whys and bothers ... enough of that! And that's how it should be yet!

You were busy all the time, you know! You had to bake bread every night. Cook your meat and bake your bread. And then skin your furs. Some nights you'd be up perhaps 'til after twelve o'clock! Then up again around four, get ready for the next day. Have breakfast and get ready. You keep all the fur just skinned, and put it in a bag and hang it outdoors all the time, until you get back to the main cabin. And then you put them out on the boards, you see. You had to be careful how you thawed your fur, too. That was something you had to be very careful about. On account of heat, eh? If there's too much heat, then it makes your furs curly, see? But if you thaw it right you don't get that. Best way is to thaw it in a bag. Put it in a cotton bag and let them thaw that way. Not too much heat, a good way from the stove.

Working hard, coming out every day. You had to travel every day. You had a lot of traps, you know. You didn't just have a day—'twas over and over, day after day. I had a lot of traps! Early in the morning, there I was, camping in my tent, or in tilt, too. You'd never let the fire go out. You'd sleep in between the fires. Then when you get up in the morning, your stuff was properly dried. Take down camp and move somewhere else. Cold, some mornings, breaking camp. Cold and cold! But it's all right, after. 'Twas cold, but after you get off hauling a little bit, you get right warm. Then you had to dig out the traps, you know. Take them out of the snow and re-set them. Lots of them! Let me see now—one, two, three...four, five, six! That was all the way round. I had six tilts. But then I had days off besides that. I might have a day off another way, you see. Back to one tilt, two nights at that place. There was al-ways...everybody, I think...had in their path, the trapline, a day off. Take a whole day to go out and come back. That was in the old marten days. In the old days when I trapped, the marten was plenty—like now. They went away. Well I s'pose there was so many trappers as well. Well, you take it, now—people trapping right from here, right over the bay, and right up, way up past Churchill Falls. Trapped right the way through—a path on one side of the river and perhaps a path on the other side—all the whole ways up, so there was a lot of fur caught. The trappers went right in to trap. Go up there 'n' boys used to go in there in September and not come out 'til the middle of January. Oh, yes! There was a lot of trapping. And a lot of fur caught, too! Lots of fur.

It must have been in about 1950 I s'pose, later than that I guess [when trapping slackened off]. About thirty-five years ago. The price of fur went down—went right down, rock bottom. Cats, lynx—everything. Went right down. That was around the Second World War, just after that, eh? That's why everybody gave it up. Couldn't do nothing with it.

Jerome: Well, what changed everything was when the fur went right down to nothing—couldn't make a living on it, see? That's the reason a lot of people were giving up, you see, because they couldn't make a living on it. Myself, I couldn't make a living on it, and keep the family, you know. I worked at it, and then, one winter, I went up the river and I got quite a bit of fur. You couldn't make no money on it, you couldn't make a living...so you had to give it up, or [starve]. The Base was here then, see, and I started working on the Base. And, in the spring of the year, they [other Settlers] would go duck hunting...and we were in there workin', and—Oh! God!—I wished the hell I was out there too, you know! (Laughs)

You get over that after a while, you know! Yes, I got over that—trapping. Oh! And then it's not so bad. I was making some good pay—not too much at the end, but it seemed like a lot of money! You could buy a lot for a little money, anyway. Now, you got to pay a lot of money for a little, eh? (Laughs)

Alfred: None of my sons ever saw it [the trapline]! The price of fur went right down. Low price, very very low—$2 for a mountain cat stick. Well, since then—I was too old to go back then. Oh, it was by far the best [way of life]! Still is for me, but I can't do nothing about it now—a man seventy-four years of age...I don't know what to say about it, but it was a wonderful life. But trap right! Go and stay in until January or sometime like that, you know. Stay all fall and come out in the winter. Go in by canoe and come back on snowshoes. No radios or nothing...like we used to go. Might get a letter once in a while, you know. If we were lucky, if someone was coming up behind you, you might get a letter in October!

Oh, yes! [People trap these days] but you can call it a little bit! That's all it is. ...You don't go off these days unless you go off on skidoo! What I think I'd rather be doing is walking! I trapped a long time. Started when I was thirteen, going with my brother, eh? That's a long time. Some years I'd get some fur, some years I'd get nothing. Everybody was like that. But most often the minks. Sometimes the marten, or the fox. Marten was a better price than a fox. Not as good as the minks, though. And martens, they were good too. But I don't know. I know nothing about it this year.

Jerome: Yes, it's like that now [people using snowmobiles]. At one time, it wasn't like that, eh? The only ones who know what it was like when you wasn't trapping with skidoo, you know—all that kind of stuff, is the people that did it. Now, you can go off on skidoo, and as long as you don't break down, it's like a pleasure trip, if the going is good—the weather and all that kind of stuff! In a couple of hours, you're up to my cabin up there! I remember going up from Red River. It took three days to get up to Naskapi River, hauling heavy loads, you know, and that's the difference!

George: No. No one goes out that far. No one uses the country now —not that far, no. No one goes in the country nowadays. No one traps for a living any more. ...

The descriptions given above highlight certain activities common to Settlers who worked traplines. It becomes apparent from the descriptions above that the trapping way of life was, and still is, appealing to the Settlers of North West River. To be associated with this tradition earns the respect of all of the Settler community, and trapping imagery is a strong element in the development of contemporary Settler identity. Several of these trapping activities have become pertinent to the social character of 'trapper.'

The older members of the community who trapped remember that differences between Indian and Settler harvesting customs were recognized and respected during the early days of trapping. For example, the main activity for the Indians was hunting rather than trapping, and vice versa for Settlers. The Indians moved over large areas in different seasons and from year to year, while the Settlers were attached to one trapline; and the Indians travelled with their families rather than alone or with other hunters.

The respect was seen by the trappers as symptomatic of a relationship of interdependence between Settlers and Indians while both groups subsisted in the country, and it was symbolized by commensality and hospitality. Settlers relied on Indians to provide tools, such as snowshoes, toboggans and crooked knives, and to prepare caribou hide for leggings, boots and mitts, all of which were essential for trapping. Indians increasingly relied on goods traded from Settlers in the country or from the posts. Supplies were limited by the fact that the journey into the country was made by canoe and foot, and it was often necessary to share these meagre supplies with others who had run short or lost their supplies through misadventure. Indians frequently traded hides and skins for food when they met trappers in the bush, and they sometimes used the Settlers they met regularly as middlemen traders, thus averting the need to travel out to a trading post.

Likewise, during the long periods spent in the country, neighbouring Indians and Settlers provided necessary support in difficult times for otherwise isolated individuals. Hospitality was important in a sparsely inhabited country, and the visits of people trapping and hunting in the vicinity were welcome highlights in an otherwise lonely existence for the trappers. The visits of 'buddies' who were on their way between the post and their camps usually meant an exchange of news and goods. Friendships often formed between Settlers and Indians who frequented the same districts in the country, and a pattern of visiting developed between neighbours in which the time of day was a less important criterion for visiting than was the proximity of a tilt or camp to a route being taken by journeying trappers and Indians.

Familiarity with this form of social interaction, and the friendships ensuing from it, have become features of the 'trapper' social character which are displayed in social interactions among Settlers in contemporary North West River. Indian 'buddies' are mentioned in conversations between individuals who wish to espouse a 'trapper' social character. In turn, the 'trapper' is seen by the other Settlers who are taking part in the social interaction as displaying an affiliation with a tradition which is important to Settler identity. Knowledge of the particular skills associated with trapping, and of 'bush' skills in general, are also discussed among those aspiring to be seen as 'trappers' in contemporary social contexts.

Settlers with trapping experience gained during the fur trade take pride in knowing how to 'trap right'—that is, without such mechanical aids as snowmobiles, aircraft and radios. This form of trapping is thought to be outmoded by those Settlers who trap for recreation nowadays, and the preference for using or not using such mechanical aids creates a distinction between the older trappers and Settlers who trap today. The older trappers mourn the loss of a way of life which has been denied to the younger members of North West River. This way of life gave the participants the opportunity to conform to a set of cultural ideals and express values which were culturally important. Cutting and working a trapline was a test of strength and endurance for young men whose lives were shaped along their fur paths, and the whole community celebrated the seasonal events and activities dictated by the trapping way of life.

By espousing the 'trapper' social character, younger community members are claiming an affiliation with the past through which they can strengthen their contemporary social identity. They lay claim to the social character through the experiences of their fathers, and also by virtue of the fact that many of them trap for recreation, acquiring some knowledge of trapping as an activity. Thus, the social character of 'trapper' can be espoused by those who did not partake in trapping as an economic activity, and, as we shall see in the following chapters, the role of the economic trapper becomes divorced from the developing social character of 'trapper.'

To encode the symbolism of the 'trapper' in social interactions, then, is to invoke sentiments about the past which define Settler identity in terms of a trapping existence, and which, through the experiences of the trapper, co-opt Indians as friends and comrades in an arena outside the community. The trappers' perceptions of Indians as friends become important in this context, and the complex nature of ethnicity in Settler social experience becomes apparent. The change in occupation, which led to a more sedentary existence for the Settlers, created changes both in their perceptions of Indians and in their relations with them. The transition from a bush-oriented, transhumant economy to segregated sedentarization is explored in the next chapter.

Bridge Apart   6

The Effects of Sedentarization
and Occupational Change on
Perceptions of Indian/Settler Relations
in North West River

Settler perceptions of Indian/Settler relations have changed as a result of the Settlers' move from a trapping way of life to a town-based lifestyle with administrative and service-oriented occupations. The change in the economic arena has affected the perceptions of both the old trappers, and the younger community members. The perceptions of the trappers reflect their former trapping lifestyle, whereas those of the younger Settlers, who have seldom experienced the social relations which went with trapping as a way of life, make no such references. The change in perception due to sedentarization, then, can be traced through the lifespan of the older members of the community when they reflect upon the differences that they perceive between the Indians of today and the Indians they once knew in the country. It can also be traced with reference to the generational differences in perception which are expressed by older members in contrast to younger members in the community.

Several consequences follow from the transfer of occupation from outside the community to within the town. The loss of the 'bush' environment as an arena for social interaction (between Settlers and Settlers, as well as between Indians and Settlers) represents one side of the change due to sedentarization. Visiting, hospitality and commensality, which were characteristic of bush life, do not occur between Indians and Settlers in town. The gaining of the town environment for social interaction represents the other side of the change.

Sedentarization for both Settlers and Indians has meant that both groups are in year-long social contact which is no longer based solely upon the shared pursuit of economic activities and the concomitant skills, which was the case in the country. In fact, the physical proximity of the two groups has, paradoxically, resulted in an increased sense of separation between Indians and Settlers. The potential for inter-group tensions has increased now that both Indians and Settlers are sedentarized year-round. Rather than becoming a combined and heterogeneous community, the two groups have sought to retain their distinct cultural identities and exaggerate their differences.

In the context of the town environment, the physical separation of the two communities (Indian and Settler) by the river also became an important symbolic separation, and the building of the bridge has focused attention on this symbolism. Whereas the possibility of conflict between these two distinct groups sharing an environment remained implicit in many of the country activities, the tensions have become much more overt within the town environment, and the bridge represents a breach in an otherwise safe boundary between the two groups.

In the conversation below, Alfred reminisces about conversing in Innu Aimun (the Cree dialect spoken in Labrador) with the Indian friends he had in the past. Since both Settlers and Indians have become sedentary, he has lost contact with these friends:

> I used to talk one time, years ago. But I can't talk to no one no more. It's different since they got [settled] ...I don't know. They seem to speak different or something. It's the same Indians, but there's some of them from Davis Inlet who speak quite a bit different — quite a lot different.1 But I talked to the old people, and they spoke different. I mean, perhaps they spoke different because it was me, eh? Because I was talking to them. But I could sit down and talk to the old people very good, you know! Anyway, I've been away from them all. I don't know any now, just a few old people. Those young people across the river, I don't even know who they are! See them in the store, that's all. Chance one will come and speak to me that I know. Old people, I can talk to them. But there's a very few left. I speak to the older ones, not the younger ones. I don't mix with them very much, you know. I don't go over there. But the old people was awful friendly, you know. Awful friendly people. If I sees them, or anything like that, [they are] awful glad to see me. Still glad to meet me. I'm glad to meet them, too! Chance time a man might come to the house to see me. I was reared up and played with them, you know. Playing all day long, only had time to eat. Shooting with the bow and arrow, and football. Then baseball, had that an awful lot. It was different then. Plenty of fish and trout, salmon.

Alfred is translating his lack of association with present-day Indians into his recent difficulty in speaking Innu Aimun. In the past both friendships and language were maintained with relative ease. He rarely sees an Indian in the community today, whereas he played with them as a child and they were bush companions when he trapped. Thus, his perceptions of old Indians differ from those he has of young Indians, and his perceptions of Indians of the past are different from those he has of the Indians of today. If these differences are examined more closely, it is possible to trace them to a difference felt in the sharing of values connected with similar occupations. Oldtimers such as Alfred developed relationships with Indians who were using the same district of the country and, to some extent, the same resources, in order to earn a living at a time when hunting and trapping were the only occupations possible for the majority of people. He "speaks to the older ones, not the younger ones" because the grounds for developing such a relationship no longer exist with the younger ones who do not, and never did, hunt in the country. His casual socializing with the 'older ones' has, for him, an element of nostalgia in reminding him of his past as an active trapper.

The point that the oldtimers' perceptions of change are based on the perceived differences between old and young Indians is supported by the following conversation with an elderly woman. Elsie was married to a trapper, and lived at Pearl River for a number of years until she and her husband and family moved to the Downalong district of North West River. She is now seventy-six and one of the community's renowned storytellers.

Each of the following pieces has as its theme the perceived change in the relationship between Indians and Settlers. The first section is a reminiscence of the past, in which Elsie describes a pattern she recognized in relationships between Settlers and Indians during her youth. This pattern involves the seasonal visiting of the Indians as they travelled between post and hunting grounds. Extolling the virtues of Indians as hard workers is inextricably linked with describing them as friends because it is equally part of the hunting and trapping lifestyle and a part which gained the respect of the Settlers as fellow toilers on the land. She also compares this past relationship with the absence of such a relationship in the present:

> When I hears the people say that the Indians don't work hard, I have seen them work terrible hard, [those] who used to come over to our house, this is before I was married, with their loads of things, and carrying their children, and hauling their children. They'd be wet sometimes, half up to the waist. The poor women, and the man besides, used to work terrible hard. I know it because I saw it. And I really like the Indians, who are really nice people. And I still do, but I'm not used to Indians now like I used to be then. Once the

Indians used to be my friends. And I still likes them yet. But I don't know how they gets along these days.

The next piece illustrates that visiting between Indians and Settlers seldom occurs in the community. Again, the distinction between the old Indians and the younger ones is made and it is with the old Indians that social contact, if any, is maintained:

> They'd stop in. Well, I also said it was in my early days, you know. Early days I was talking about. Yes, but those later days I don't know nothing about those Indians, I never see them. But real often, there used to be a wonderful old lady, she used to come round and see me down there [Pearl River] and sew and do everything in the house and even have the supper cooked, and all that kind of thing. But I never sees that up here [North West River]. Poor things, they're all dead. [I] don't know the younger ones.

The final piece gives Elsie's perception of the younger Indians, and the resultant lack of social contact between Settlers and Indians:

> Then the government gives 'em help. Well, what a thing! Then all they have to go on drinking, and they bring a whole lot of beer. All this stuff from Goose Bay, just to give 'em a go. Sell for a big price. And all [of] them drunk. And, oh heavens! That's all I hears about them now and I don't even ask about them! But you could see them dressed up and ready to come across. They used to. Don't even see them now, I don't get over and see them anyway!

Elsie's description of the younger Indians emphasizes the contrast which is perceived to exist between relations with the older Indians and relations with the younger ones. The relationship between Settlers and Indians in the country developed from a point of common interest in a lifestyle or occupation. This point of common interest is precisely what is missing in Elsie's description of the young Indians of the present. These segments of conversation from oldtimers in the community show that they perceive a change in the relationship between themselves and Indians which has occurred during their lifetime. The next few segments of conversation will attempt to show that generational differences in perception have also arisen as a result of sedentarization.

The following conversation introduces a person from the generation after that of Alfred and Elsie. Rita is in her fifties and has spent most of her life working for the International Grenfell Association as an auxiliary nursing aide. Her husband began his working life as a trapper but soon gave this up and has worked steadily in a series of government departments associated with the care and maintenance of Crown Lands. Here, Rita is talking about the visiting she engaged in as a child, and compares it to the lack of visiting done by present-day children in the community:

> Oh! Gosh, yes! We'd go more them days than they would now. Glad to see the Indians! They were really good, eh? We'd go over a lot more than they do now! [They] used to sell deerskin shoes, and make things. Whatever they had made, you know, snowshoes 'n' stuff, [they would sell]. They weren't really our friends. They were more our father's friends, eh? They trapped with my father, eh? That's all! So, old [Indian] trappers used to come down from their trapping grounds and come up along the lake where I was, you know. [They would] always come in, in the house, and have a cup of tea. They were pretty clean, them days. Much cleaner than what they are now. Well, some clean ones, some not so clean.

The conversation shows several things. Firstly, like many other Settlers of her generation, Rita mentions that the Indians visiting and being visited were her father's friends. Therefore her reminiscences of visits between Settlers and Indians are from her childhood when the social contact was maintained by her father. Social contact by proxy (through parents), then, is considered by the children of oldtimers to be a form of relationship with the Indians, and so the social character of 'trapper' can be espoused by more people than just those who are trappers.

Secondly, the remark: "We'd go over a lot more than they do now" suggests that this form of social contact (by proxy) is one that does not exist in the present: 'We' (as youngsters) would visit a lot more than 'they' (the youngsters of today) visit. People of Rita's generation have some perception of Indians as friends through the contacts that their parents maintained. Such contacts by proxy do not exist for members of younger generations whose parents never had such social contact with Indians.

Rita is also describing childhood visits she paid to the Indians who were camped across the river. During this part of her life Rita lived in Upalong with her family. She recalls a period when Settlers from around the Hamilton Inlet region were moving to North West River, but the Indians were still nomadic and visited North West River only in the summer. Visits were welcomed as much because they were a form of entertainment for the Settlers, as they were because the purchase of goods was anticipated.

A yet more striking cleavage in inter-generational perceptions is found when talking to the generation represented by Rita's children. This generation, which consists of the adolescents and school children of present-day North West River, has no memory of the social patterns of life in the country. In order to explain this striking change in perception more clearly, I shall turn to another example, taken from the transcript of a discussion held at a meeting of the recently re-formed North West River United Church Youth Group.[2] At the time of the discussion, the Youth Group comprised members from most sectors in the North West River community, mainly because it was a new and novel social event and so all the eligible youngsters in the community sought to attend meetings during this initial period of the club's operation. There were few other forms of social activity open to this age group in the community at the time, and outdoor activities were severely inhibited by the inclement January weather.

The meetings had developed a pattern whereby they began with organized activity of some sort, followed by a period of discussion on a selected theme. This procedure was followed on this particular occasion. A formal, or planned, discussion took place on the theme of 'racism,' primarily because of my presence in the group.[3] The theme of racism was taken up by the Youth Group leader, who prepared a set of questions to encourage the discussion. Although questions of any kind can act to inhibit a free discussion or shape the responses of participants, these questions posed initially to the group very soon became irrelevant, such was the strength of feeling about the subject of Indians. The discussion period began according to a prescribed format[4] which led to a general debate. The section of transcription below starts with a member reading out a question at the beginning of the general discussion:

Maria: Question: Name four ways of downplaying or eliminating racism, if you had such a problem in your community.

Danny: Use the same school![5]

Mary (leader): What would happen, the first couple of days, if everyone got together in the same school?

Ken and several others: Everybody'd have a big fight! After a few days everybody would ignore them.

Others: Ignore them!

Mary: Why?

Several: Because we don't like them!

Mary: Why don't you like them?

Sheana: I don't know!

Danny: You guys [the girls] don't like 'em 'cause we don't like them!

Mary: Who would start the fight?

Ken: We would!

Darlene and several others: They would.

Ken: We don't know! It would develop.

Mary: It develops because, what? You hate each other?

Several: No ...

John: We don't get along together.

Mary: Why don't you get along?

Bridget: Racism.

Darlene: Because they're Indians and we're not!

Several: Because they're different.

Mary: They're different?

Ken: And we're not! (Laughter.)

John: They're different from us and we're different from them.

Lucy: My Mum told me not to play with them (tongue in cheek).[6]
             (Laughter.)

Mary: So therefore you can't get along because you're different?
             Right?

John: Not really, we just don't want to get along.

Danny: Yeah, we'd get along if we wanted to!

Mary: So the problem, basically, is that you don't want to get
             along?

Ken and others: Right!

Darlene: You've got it!

Barry: They stick to their ways and we stick to ours.

Mary: So you can't mix because you're different?

Barry: No. We didn't say that. We can mix, but it's not much use.

Ken: We can mix if we want, but we don't want to!

Danny: We don't have no reason to.

Evie: Why is there no reason to mix?

Ken: What reasons are there?

Evie: Because you live in the same part of Labrador ...

Ken: That's no reason!

Danny: But we don't belong to the same town.

Mary: You are neighbours.

John: But we don't live in the same town. We don't go to the same school...

Sheana: They are all across the river.

Danny: What reason do we have for going over there?

Ken: What reason do they have for coming over here?

Mary: What reason do you have for becoming the friend of anyone in this youth group?

Danny: I don't know!

Mary: Because it's kind of good to have friends, isn't it?

Several: Yeah!

Danny and others: Because we were brought up together!

Ken: Yeah! We were brought up together.

All: We were raised here. We were brought up here. They were raised over there.

Mary: Okay, you guys. Take this example: There is this gorgeous girl who moves into town and she is *nice!*

Ken and boys: Wow! Hot, man!

Mary: She was raised, let's say England. She didn't have anything in common with you. She lived over there. ...

Several: She would live in this community, not across the river!

Danny: Let's hear the story!

Mary: Okay. She moved into this community and she had nothing in common with you except that she now lives in North West River and so do you. And the fact she's a gorgeous female. ...Are you going to get to know her?

Chorus from boys: Yeah!

Danny: But no one over there is gorgeous.

Ken: Yes they are! Still no reason to go over.

Mary: Okay, but you've just told me you can't get along with those over there because you've got nothing in common! You could get along with that gorgeous female!

Several: Yeah!

John: That's because you want to, there's something to get along for!

Danny: There's interest!

Ken: No!...there's something you want!

Tim: No, there's a barrier between us...like, eh...

Ken: The bridge!

Danny: There's a barrier between us.

Mary: What kind of barrier?

Barry: Hostilities!

Ken: Hostility through the ages!

Mary: So you guys are telling me that you have to stick to tradition all the time and if tradition is hostility, you're not going to change it?

Barry: No, not really. Not really....

Several: Not really.

The general argument running through the discussion soon becomes tautological, but, in relation to other discussions that the group has had, in which the usual response is slow, this discussion serves to show an extraordinary amount of hostile feeling. It becomes apparent that there is a great deal of peer pressure being exerted by the group upon individual participants in the discussion. This gives rise to a 'team spirit,' and the formation of a 'team North West River' social character. The children are drawn into increasing statements of mutual support against the outsiders or other team, which, in this case, is represented by the Indians. Danny's statement that the girls are hostile towards the Indians because the boys in their peer group are hostile is an illustration of this pressure to conform. The 'team North West River' social character comes into play also in debates about Rigolet, a neighbouring Settler community to the east, which has been considered a rival of North West River since its inception during the pioneer period in the history of settlement in Hamilton Inlet.[7] It is also espoused by adults in their discussions about North West River as a community in opposition to other communities in Labrador. Notably, Settlers engaging in discussions about the secession of Sheshatshit espouse the 'team North West River' social character in an attack on the decision taken by the Indian community, a decision which is seen as hostile to North West River.

The further separation of Indians and Settlers into the distinct communities of North West River and Sheshatshit occurred within the lifetime of the Youth Group generation, and there are not even the old Indian acquaintances of parents through which to remember the social interactions of the trapping way of life. Far from recollecting occasional summer visits to the Indians across the river, these children have a cognitive picture of separation between Indians and Settlers which certainly inhibits visiting. This sense of the separateness between Sheshatshit and North West River also preceded the division of the former community.[8] As the unknown territory of the neighbouring town, Sheshatshit is full of mystery and instils fear into the children of North West River. I would often be teased about 'getting lost' if I crossed into the unknown territory across the bridge.

The example cited below illustrates the absence of visiting between younger Settlers and Indians, and represents an interesting example of many similar instances when the topic of visiting across the river was discussed.

Early on a winter's evening as I was on my way to visit Indian friends living across the river I was joined on my walk along the main road in North West River by a young Settler, Pam, a thirteen-year old who lives in Upalong. We talked about the weather and the activities of the Youth Group, although Pam was a few months too young to become a member. She showed surprise and interest when she discovered that I planned to visit in Sheshatshit, and said that she would come with me. We resumed our talk of the Youth Group and other social events in the community until we reached the centre of town. Then Pam asked me more questions about who I was visiting and why, asking whether I really intended to walk across the bridge and through Sheshatshit on my own in the dark. I replied by asking whether she was still interested in accompanying me, and she giggled and looked shocked. She said that she had no intention of crossing the bridge with me, and that she had never been on that side of the river anyway. As we approached the bridge, which is where we would take separate directions to reach Sheshatshit and Upalong, she attempted to persuade me to visit people in Upalong with her, as I had often done, rather than carry on across the bridge. When I responded by trying to persuade her to visit across the bridge with me, Pam ran off into the bushes at the side of the road to hide, shouting that she was too scared to even go near the bridge, let alone walk across it to Sheshatshit. I continued across the bridge on my own.

There are several points to be made about this interaction. The bridge and the area around the bridge is a place fraught with meaning for most members of the community. There are many reasons for this. The bridge has meaning because it is the place of geographical contact with the neighbouring community of Sheshatshit which is otherwise cut off from North West River by water. However, the symbolism of the bridge will be discussed more fully below, and I shall return here to Pam's response to the idea of visiting in Sheshatshit. I want to make two points about this. Firstly, the idea of visiting with people in Sheshatshit, or with Indians at all, is alien to her. Secondly, the idea of visiting on the other side of the river is also threatening to her. This is not only because it is a visit to a neighbouring community with which there might be some sense of rivalry, but because the bridge represents the breach in an otherwise 'secure' boundary between the two communities. This is a reversal of the idea prevalent in the oldtimers' perceptions of the past: that visiting was the focus of Settler and Indian social interaction and was the main way of displaying hospitality.

The site of the river crossing is a complex part of the community's geography. It is both the economic and social centre of the community, and the interface between North West River and Sheshatshit. It is one of the few places in North West River where Settlers are likely to meet with Indians, being a 'no man's land' outside the domain of either. Since the bridge was built, the ambiguity around this part of town has increased.

The bridge was built in anticipation of a road to be built between Happy Valley-Goose Bay and Makkovik. This road had been intended to facilitate the mining and removal of uranium which had been found to the west of Makkovik.[9] Although residents of North West River and Sheshatshit had been offered a choice of sites for the bridge (either the present location which is directly between the two communities, or at the 'Rapids' which separate Grand Lake and Little Lake), there was little choice about whether there would be a bridge or not. In fact, the decision to build a bridge was initially welcomed by most of the Settlers to whom I spoke. The misgivings came later. On the other hand, the Indian community (not surprisingly) was never in favour of the building of the bridge at either site.

Before the bridge was built, people would often exchange pleasantries whilst waiting for the cable car, and before the advent of the cable car people used a ferrying system which required co-operation for sharing canoes; Settlers ferried people from the north bank south and Indians ferried people from the south bank north. The bridge requires neither co-operation nor the social contact which is likely to ensue from such co-operation. Thus nowadays it is possible to pass people on the bridge and not acknowledge their presence at all. It is also interesting to note that the building of the bridge coincided with the secession of Sheshatshit from North West River. In the act of seceding, the inhabitants of Sheshatshit expressed a desire to be considered an independent community, thereby dispensing with the need for the nominal communication between the two communities which was required when the two groups acted as one municipality. Similarly, having the bridge as a means by which to cross the river also did away with the need for nominal communication.

In recent years, the bridge has been the site of 'rock fights' between the children of North West River and Sheshatshit. These short-lived skirmishes between Indian and Settler children occur in the summer, and Settler children have boasted of them to me on a number of different occasions. It is significant that the oldtimers recall from their childhood summer activities such as playing football and wrestling with Indian children. These activities, which also took place at the site on which the present bridge is built, have given way to rock fights in this generation.

Returning for a moment to the transcript of the Youth Group, there is one final point I wish to make. It concerns the children's perception that the barrier they perceive between themselves and the Indians arises from "hostilities through the ages." This contradicts the memories of the old trappers who remember friendships made through extending and accepting hospitality in the bush environment. The significance of this contradiction is two-fold, and it brings together the points made above. There is a marked difference between the social behaviours of people in the confines of the community and outside the community in the 'bush.' There is also a marked difference in perception which is related to occupational changes and to concurrent changes in the situation of the individual in relation to the broader situational changes of the community.

Sedentarization has changed the nature of Indian/Settler relations by changing the arena of social and economic activities from the bush to the town. Paradoxically, rather than providing greater opportunity for social interaction between Settlers and Indians, the year-round proximity brought about by the sedentarization of both Settlers and Indians has caused a decline in social interactions, and the two groups have become more distant. The bridge has become a symbol of the change which has occurred with the transfer of economic and social activities from the country to the community. The effect that the resulting change in perceptions has had on the development of social characters is three-fold. Firstly, those Settlers who trapped as an economic activity carry with them the perceptions that developed from the relationships that they maintained with Indians while they were trapping and hunting away from the town. These perceptions are no longer appropriate to the situation which has developed within the community, in which there is a lack of social interaction between Settlers and Indians. In response to the change, the old trappers have developed a new set of perceptions of the young Indians who live in Sheshatshit. The relationship that the old trappers have with these young Indians, this new set of perceptions, has become part of the social character of 'trapper.' Thus, as the old trappers have become detached from their past experiences in the role of economic trapper, so they have espoused the social character of 'trapper' in its stead.

Secondly, at the same time that the social character of 'trapper' has become detached from the actual trapper through the transference of economic activities from trapping to the sedentary occupations of the town, the social character of the 'trapper' has become the property of Settlers other than those who were *bona fide* trappers. Those Settlers whose parents trapped claim the status of 'trapper by proxy,' and these Settlers espouse the social character of 'trapper' by displaying an appreciation of trapping which they have gained from their parents. To a lesser extent, Settlers can also espouse the social character of 'trapper' by virtue of having had some trapping experience through their own present-day recreational activities as trappers.

Thirdly, since occupations which have arisen within the community are of a different nature to those which occurred in the bush, the levels of social interaction possible between Settlers and Indians are also different. Younger members of the community have different perceptions of Indian/Settler relations which have arisen from the different nature of social interaction between Settlers and Indians in town. Substantive social characters have yet to emerge from the experiences of the young community members, although peer pressure does have the effect of causing the youngsters to share two perceptions: (1) that the community of Sheshatshit is in opposition to their community, and (2) that the culture of the Indian residents of Sheshatshit is alien in comparison to their culture.

I have not fully analyzed the paradox that increased physical proximity has increased social distance between the two groups, nor have I been able to explore the full meaning of the part that the bridge plays in this paradox. This paradox needs more attention at some future date. What I hope to have done is to have shown that the paradox exists, and that it has significantly altered Indian/Settler relations, and hence, Settlers' perceptions of Indian/Settler relations. The alterations in Indian/Settler relations and Settler perceptions thereof are reflected in the development of the social character of 'trapper,' as well as in the traits of the social characters which arise in opposition to the 'trapper'—namely the 'newcomer,' the youngsters' 'team North West River,' and social characters which pertain to the local elite. We shall explore this in the next chapter.

Upalong–Downalong

*The Effect of Differences in
Occupation upon Social Organization
and the Formation of Social Characters
in North West River*

In this chapter, the pattern of residence within the town, which was explored in Chapter Three, becomes the starting point for the exploration of the community's segmentary nature, and the resulting social characters of 'Upalonger' and 'Downalonger.' To recapitulate, the present-day town of North West River is divided into residential sections which represent groups of kin and, to some extent, reflect the earlier pattern of settlement found along the shores of Lake Melville. Land granted originally to individual Settlers when they moved to North West River has since been divided up among their descendants, and the clusters of houses which occupy single land grants are often found to belong to brothers, sisters, parents, children and other relatives. Land grants have also been shared among families related through marriage, and adjacent plots of land often house people originally from neighbouring settlements along the Lake Melville shore. Residential areas in the community, then, have formed into enclaves of kin and networks of friends, although the inhabitants of North West River superficially form one community.

Social status can be measured by place of residence since the formation of enclaves based on kinship has facilitated more than just the selective inheriting and sharing of land. Access to economic security and to prestigious occupations which confer status and power in the community are controlled and manipulated through kin-groups and networks, which limit access to resources and opportunities to a few inhabitants while others seldom profit.

Patronage, in the form of selective job opportunities, reached its peak during the reign of the International Grenfell Association in North West River. As we have seen, the IGA began its operations by recruiting professional staff from abroad, and supplementing this staff with workers drawn from the communities in which it operated.

The Association's patronage was granted to certain families in these communities for a variety of reasons. Once members of the community were favoured by the Association, they were able to safeguard employment opportunities for themselves and their fellow kin-group members. In its early days, the Mission in North West River was not solely the provider of various services, but was also the focus for many different forms of development in the region. Grenfell entertained businessmen, explorers and the ambassadors of wealthy families in his attempts to develop Labrador. As a dynamic force for development, the International Grenfell Association controlled interests in a number of activities, and so it wielded considerable influence. This meant that, even if jobs (and hence security) were not forthcoming with the Association itself, jobs elsewhere in the community were to be had with the backing of the Mission. Thus, nowadays, families which have members working for the International Grenfell Association seem also to have members involved in other prestigious activities in the community (for instance, the running of stores and government offices and other businesses).

The patronage system set up by the International Grenfell Association was responsible for the formation of underprivileged groups in the community as well as for the creation of an elite (which was, and still is, regularly supplemented by various incoming professionals). Recently, the elite has become involved in political activities which entail the manipulation of Settler ethnic identity. As local politicians, the elite are trying to mobilize Settlers as 'Labradorians' in order to gain access to Federal Government sympathies. At the same time, some of the less privileged groups in the community have come to represent a more traditional Settler identity, such as 'trapper' and 'oldtimer,' which the local politicians wish to mobilize (to form the substance of a 'Labradorian,' and therefore distinctly Settler, identity). Association with the different parts of town has become integral to the evolution of these groups, the members of which are, in turn, vested with certain perceptions, thus forming a number of social characters.

Since the staff of the International Grenfell Association and the Hudson's Bay Company were frequently given housing close to the centre of town on land which was granted to the Association and Company, many of the community's elite live here. The town expands from this central point, following the river bank upstream along the shore of Little Lake, to Upalong, and downstream along the edge of Lake Melville, to Downalong. Upalong is a relatively small section of the town, whereas Downalong can be divided into a number of residential areas. Some of these areas are less relevant than others in the social structure of the community, yet most represent the hubs of kin-groups. Of the residential sections in the community, Upalong and Downalong are the most frequently mentioned and, in terms of community social structure, Upalongers and Downalongers form mutually exclusive groups. As we have seen in Chapter Four, these kin-groups devolved from the family of one of the first pioneers to settle in Hamilton Inlet and their devolution into separate kin-groups has facilitated the differentiation of past experiences between the two groups.

Upalongers have become the marked case.[1] It is among the Upalongers that the only marriages between Indians and Settlers in North West River have taken place; two Indian women are presently married to Upalong men, and both families live in Upalong. Upalongers do not constitute a powerful group in the community; they have no representation on the Town Council or other political groups, nor are there entrepreneurs amongst them, except for one man who runs a small convenience store.[2]

During the period of the fur trade, Upalongers ran traplines at various points along the inland waterways of the Hamilton River and Grand Lake, and are frequently mentioned in the Hudson's Bay Company journals of the time. Many Upalong oldtimers are well-known for their trapping and prospecting exploits during the time of the fur trade and the development of the Labrador interior. Stories of their renown have added greatly to the contemporary image of the trapping way of life. Of these oldtimers, a good number continued to trap at least part-time after the decline of trapping as the community's main economic activity, and have stopped only as a result of infirmity and old age. Upalongers have seldom found employment with the International Grenfell Association to supplement their bush-related incomes.

Downalongers entertain distinct perceptions about Upalongers. These perceptions are both positive and negative, and thus flexible · to social advantage. In general terms, Downalongers see Upalongers as people who understand the trapping way of life, who have woodsman skills and who have not completely made the transition from a trapping economy to wage labour. Downalongers and Upalongers both see Downalongers as those who have made a successful transition from a trapping economy to a wage economy, and therefore as people who have surrendered their knowledge of the land for more prestigious occupations with steady hours and a secure income. As will be seen below, Downalongers also consider the traits which to a large extent characterize Upalongers as being intrinsically Indian traits. Thus, Downalongers see Upalongers as being culturally identifiable with Indians in some situations, and this is a perception which Upalongers reject.

Several things arise from this pattern of segregated identities. Upalongers in contemporary North West River are assumed, by Downalongers, to have a higher level of skills pertaining to the bush environment. They are frequently called upon for their skills as woodsmen and knowledge of the woods. An example of this assumption occurred at a meeting of the Town Council which I attended. The Council had made plans for a 'make-work' project to be implemented during the following spring season. It involved cutting and clearing a track through part of the surrounding countryside to make cabins more accessible. The availability of certain Upalongers for the work became an integral part of the planning for this project. It was argued that these Upalongers were the best woodcutters in the community and, if the project were to be well executed, they should be employed. It was not known when the Upalongers would be available to work on the project, and some thought was given to the problem of making the implementation of the project coincide with the availability of these workers.

Today a trapping lifestyle exists for only a handful of older community members who have never stopped trapping, and there are as many of these people in Downalong as in Upalong. While the majority of Upalongers do not live in a trapping economy or experience trapping as a way of life, the group is nevertheless seen by other Settlers as embodying a specifically Settler culture which is being lost. Thus, for other community members the Upalongers have become representative of a colourful past, images of which are in the process of being mobilized in the symbolism of the present-day local politicians. (*Them Days* magazine is an example of the mobilization of trapping images with the aim of strengthening Settler identity.) Upalongers are, however, the bastions of a declining Settler culture not necessarily from choice, but rather because of the relative lack of job opportunities afforded them.

Upalongers' association with the land and land-based occupations links them not only to the trapping lifestyle of the past, but also to the bush-oriented lifestyle of Indians. During my visits around North West River, when I asked for information about trapping experiences and for stories about how trappers got along with Indians in the country, I was frequently redirected to an Upalonger. I was told by Downalongers that "they all speak Indian up there (in Upalong)" and had plenty of stories about the Indians. Community members who were, or who had been, employed as

firefighters also explained to me that Indians made the best firefighters because (like Upalongers) they were good woodsmen and
knew how to act in the bush, where to fell trees and the like, but
that they were unreliable and not always available for work. These
firefighters assumed that Indians were seldom recruited by the
firefighting service because of this same unreliability.[3] Comments
like: "they can't seem to hold their drink" were repeatedly made by
other community members about both Indians and certain
Upalongers.

Upalongers, then, both augment traditional Settler cultural
identity and threaten its integrity through their perceived shared
identity with the Indians of today. The 'Indian-like' identity that
Downalongers perceive Upalongers to possess becomes an ethnic
identity within the broader Settler ethnic identity, and it is the
Indian-like elements that can become stigmatized. In response,
Upalongers attempt to draw themselves back into the broader
Settler community by alternately rejecting the 'Indian' role attributed to them and attempting to play it as a useful social strategy,
as we shall see in Chapter Eight.

The distinction between Upalong and Downalong creates fertile
ground for the formation of social characters in the community.
Downalongers perceive Upalongers as having certain traits, and
these perceptions push and trap the Upalonger into the social
character of 'Upalonger.' An example of this can be drawn from my
fieldwork.

Shortly after Christmas, I was passing the community hall when
people leaving after a dance attracted my attention. On entering the
hall, I noticed that there had been fighting, the remains of which
were still in progress when I entered. An Indian couple, fighting in
the porch of the hall, stopped as I approached and came into the
hall with me. A Settler from the 'Eskimo End' of town was standing
up with his shirt torn and his nose bleeding, waving a half empty
beer bottle in the air. The bar licence had been granted through the
Lion's Club which had opened in the community just after Sheshatshit had separated from North West River, and a few of the Lion's
Club committee members, a majority of whom were from Downalong, were escorting some Indians out. Troublesome Settlers from
both Upalong and Downalong were being encouraged to leave by
their friends and family members, and there were general attempts
to clear the hall. I noticed comparatively few fights between Indians
and Settlers at the dance. Most were between Settlers and Settlers,
with a few between Indians and Indians.

People were standing round in groups amongst scattered chairs and tables littered with beer bottles. The groups mostly consisted of onlookers, but there were a few aggressors and every now and then a fight would flare up. I was standing with some Downalong friends and neighbours, with their relatives, when a fight ensued between four women in our group. At first the fight was between two women; two others intercepted, taking sides, then joining the fight. The women yelled at each other, three taking sides against the fourth. When the three began to attack the fourth physically, several others in the group pulled them apart by wrapping their arms round the women's torsos, pinning their arms to their sides, and lifting them away from each other. The intercepters this time were male friends of the women involved, and an Upalong woman who was not part of the group. The fighting women were addressed by their intercepters with comments such as: "enough is enough," "stop being so bitchy," "calm down," "get on home and sleep it off."

Nearby, I saw a fight between two Indian girls being intercepted by an old Upalong man whose voice could not be heard above the noise. He was shortly joined by some of the Lion's Club members who were organizers of the dance. Between them, they lifted the girls from the floor, and put them out into the porch. This was no easy feat, as the girls, intent on finishing their fight, resisted and grabbed at anyone or anything to anchor themselves. Most of the comments made by the intercepters in this case were addressed to each other rather than to the aggressors:

"Take them to the porch, Bill. Let's get them out of here!"

To the girls, they said very little except for comments like "Now, now!"

Another fight began between an Indian woman and an Upalong woman. This was intercepted by women relatives of the Settler, and all comments were addressed to her. The style of these comments was not uncommon in everyday interactions between the same people, only, in this situation they were said with more vehemence:

"Ya blood of a bitch, cut it out will you! Stubborn whore, come on home!"

Later, when a group of Upalongers were leaving the hall, they found their way blocked by an Indian woman who had passed out in front of the door. One of the women in the group came forward and said:

"Excuse me! This is how you get out...walk right over, like the sidewalk!"

And she walked over the prostrate woman in order to get out.

There is a noticeable pattern in the way that the fights had been managed, and two aspects of this pattern are pertinent to my analysis. Firstly, the fights were intercepted by different people in different situations: fights between Settlers were intercepted by family members or friends, and fights between Indians, and between Indians and Settlers, were intercepted either by Upalongers, or by the organizers of the dance. Secondly, the interactions between the intercepters and the aggressors varied according to the ethnic origins of the fighters: while the intercepters spoke directly to the fighting Settlers, they did not do so to Indians. Language difference may provide part of the reason for this, but does not necessarily explain why comments about the Indians and addressed to other Settlers should be derogatory, as in the comment likening the Indian woman to a sidewalk.

The fight at the dance shows how Upalongers act when they are put in a situation which reinforces the perception of other community members that they possess a high degree of Indianness. The role of intercepter put these Upalongers in close contact with both Indians and Settlers in their conflicts, and demanded that they mediate. They were regarded as being well qualified to mediate because they are thought to share some characteristics with Indians. The response of the intercepters was to diffuse the situation, both in the physical sense of being intercepter, and in re-establishing which side of the Settler/Indian boundary they were on. While the rest of the community expressed the feeling that the Upalong intercepters were closer to the community's perception of Indianness, the intercepters made sure that they expressed allegiance with the other Settlers in the situation, and not with the Indians. The intercepters communicated directly with Settlers, which they rarely did with Indians, and the comments addressed to the Settlers made them into allies. For example, the woman who left the hall solved the problem of the blocked door from the point of view of a Settler who wished to get out, rather than from the point of view of the prostrate Indian, who needed to be lifted out of the way.

The problem of showing allegiance to Settlers rather than to Indians becomes acute for the children of Indian/Settler marriages in Upalong. Two instances from my fieldwork illustrate this point. While gathering genealogical information about the community, I met with a group of North West River high school students who had collected their family trees for a class on local history. One of the students, whose mother was Indian, had chosen to compile only that portion of her family tree containing her Settler ancestry, thus rejecting her affiliation with Indians in favour of her Settler identity among her Settler class-mates. In addition, I discovered that the perpetrators of the 'rock fights' that occurred between Indian and

Settler children (Chapter Six) were the children from the mixed marriages, who chose to show their allegiance to Settler culture by throwing rocks at the Indian children coming across the bridge. It seems that the closer a person is to direct association with Indians and Indianness, the harder it becomes to manage an ethnic identity which shares traits with Indians and Indianness.

Upalongers are caught by the perceptions of other Settlers in the social character of 'Upalonger.' They are the retainers of an ethnic identity rather than its brokers, and are thus not as able to manipulate certain cultural traits as are the brokers of the identity. As can be seen in the following excerpt from an interview I conducted, 'Indianness' is borne as a stigma by Upalongers, while it is seen by the elite as part of Settler cultural identity:

Evie: You were telling me what you felt about being Metis?

Jerome: About being Indian or Eskimo? That's right! I always said that, and I told lots of them on the Base about that—if they're going to call me Indian or Eskimo, treat me like one! I wouldn't have to pay no taxes, working for the American or Canadian Government. And they call me Indian or Eskimo! I said, if you treat me like one, you can call me anything you want to! That's true, that is!

Evie: You mean that you'd have certain rights or privileges?

Jerome: Yeah, well, I'm a white person! And I wants to be respected that way. If they call me Indian or Eskimo, they disqualify me down from my own to another grade, let's say. And if they're going to put me in that category, Okay! Don't charge me no tax, and I'll live with that as long as I live.

Evie: You wouldn't mind that?

Jerome: Not a damned bit, because I wouldn't have to pay no taxes! Whatever money I make, I wouldn't have to pay no tax! And who's going to grumble about paying no taxes? You? Eh?

Perceptions espoused by the community's elite are of a different nature. The elite are the politically active members of the community, who are in the process of establishing a distinct Settler cultural identity in which Indians are seen as allies. They perceive themselves as belonging to a culture possessing an Indianness which is permitted as a result of their past cultural contact with Indians, and which is exclusive to Settlers as Labradorians, giving the Settler population legitimate rights in Labrador. The following extract from an interview I held with an entrepreneur and one-time councillor in the community illustrates this point:

> We did [have native status as a community] at one time ... this was all native at one time. We were all natives — all the people of this area was natives. When it came to the government to collect taxes, then they turned around and said we were white Settlers. I think that a majority of people in this area — long time Settlers here — are partly native, and I feel that we do have some reason to have some part-native status. ...

Local politicians and entrepreneurs are more able to reject the stigma attached to Indianness because of their economically and politically secure positions in the community. As the brokers of ethnicity, therefore, they can choose when to espouse a traditional Settler identity because it is not, for them, stigmatized and it does not trap them into the same set of perceptions and responses as it does Upalongers.

The example given below shows how the social characters espoused by the local political elite shape their interactions amongst themselves and with Indians. It is again drawn from events taking place during a Christmas gathering. This time the party took place in the Town Hall offices and was for all municipal workers and other users of the Town Hall building. As was no doubt anticipated, some guests became drunk and caused confrontational situations. The first of these was perpetrated by an Upalonger who, after persisting in his attentions to various women, was summarily asked to leave, and escorted from the premises. This resolution of the situation was in contrast to the resolution of a similar situation involving an Indian woman, which occurred later.

I was sitting and talking with two Settler friends (an Upalonger and a Downalonger), when the woman, who was known to us all, approached us. Josephine was noticeably drunk, her movements were clumsy and her speech was impaired. She pointed to me and said:

"Hey, you! My friend. I want to talk to you!"

The Upalong woman with me turned to Josephine, aggressively telling her to go away and not be so rude, because I was already involved in a conversation which she had interrupted. Josephine replied to this by addressing the three of us with the statement:

"I hate you!"

At this point, the other Settler, a Downalong man, recommenced the conversation, addressing me and the other Settler but ignoring the Indian, who left us after a little while.

I watched several interactions between Josephine and other

people. Her interactions were mainly with people with whom she was familiar, and who were invariably members of the Downalong elite and outsiders. She addressed them in a manner similar to that which she had previously used in addressing my group, reaffirming friendships and then declaring that Indians hated whites, and that the people whom she was addressing hated her. Their response was usually to reassure her that they were friends with her and did not hate her. During these interactions, I overheard several comments from bystanding Settlers, mostly Upalongers, to the effect that the Indian woman should be evicted from the party.

Later the party thinned out, leaving a small group composed of the organizers, who were drawn almost exclusively from the community's Downalong and outsider elite, and a few of their friends and acquaintances. By this time, Josephine's interactions had become more tense. She approached one Settler woman saying:

"You hate me!," and started to cry.

The woman she had approached took her to a quiet alcove in the hall and tried to pacify her by reaffirming friendship and assuring her that her problems were understood. The Indian woman was only briefly pacified by this and similar interactions.

While these interactions were taking place, the remaining participants, including myself, had seated themselves in another alcove and were chatting about Labrador. We began a game, taking turns to ask obscure questions about Labrador, and debating various answers. Josephine joined this group. By now, she showed a very aggressive manner, hitting the people she approached, and yelling at them at close range:

"I hate you, whites!"

The members of the group carried on with the game, even addressing the people who were being attacked by the Indian woman, as if nothing was happening. Eventually, a member of the remaining group lost his temper, and grabbed hold of the woman's wrists, shouting:

"Now that's enough!"

Immediately, the attention of the whole group was on the scene. Josephine stopped her rantings, and the angered person relaxed his hold on her wrists, telling her that she should go home and 'sleep it off.' Several offers to see her safely home ensued, and were discussed among the assembled group. Someone drove her home, and so the evening ended.

The set of social interactions described above is quite different from the interactions encountered in the description of the dance, revealing that there are different perceptions at play. In this instance, the distance between Settlers and Indians is underplayed by the Settler participants. As local politicians and managers of ethnic identity, the Settlers perceive Indians as allies, and as the administrators of social and medical and educational services, the Settlers perceive Indians as their wards and clients (in much the same way as the IGA had originally perceived Settlers). In the social characters of 'ally,' 'guardian' and 'patron,' the Settlers in the situation can do very little to stop the disruption. However, when someone does attempt to confront Josephine with her disruptive behaviour, the other participants are anxious to see how the situation is handled. Although relief is felt when it is diffused, the loss of temper is not seen as an acceptable trait for the social character of 'guardian' espoused here. And so this method of handling the situation is soon dropped, and Josephine is once again extended the protective custody of her patrons and allies.

Social situations, then, bring about the espousal of social characters which appear appropriate for the individual—in their own or in *others'* eyes, in particular social contexts. The individual is, to some extent, trapped into social characters by the expectations of fellow community members. Even so, the person is still able to manipulate ethnic identity by responding selectively to social characters. Upalong Settlers are able to manipulate the 'Upalonger' social character to their advantage only when the Indian qualities of Upalongers symbolize Settler identity. They try to maintain an ethnic distance from Indians when these same qualities equate them with Indians rather than with Settlers. Downalongers (more specifically the Downalong elite), on the other hand, strengthen their ethnic identity by empathizing with Indians in their role as a politically active native group. They do this by assuming the roles of patron and guardian towards Indians, who pose no threat to the Downalongers' social identity.

Two issues have been dealt with here: the first is the relative rigidity of certain social characters, and the second is the way in which elements of an identity can become stigmatized. As social characters represent the different experiences of different sectors of the community, not all elements of all social characters are universally shared by all Settlers. In the case of the 'Upalonger' social character, certain traits which compose that character are stigmatized by other Settlers, and the interchange of 'Upalonger' with other social characters often becomes defensive on the part of the stigmatized 'Upalonger.' The espousal of some social characters, therefore, is seen as less desirable than the espousal of other social characters, and all social characters are to some extent limiting in their ability to be manipulated, as can be seen by the traits of the 'Downalonger' social character.

The 'Upalonger' social character represents an ethnic identity within the more general and pervasive Settler ethnic identity. Elements of the Settler ethnic identity have assumed negative connotations, but at the same time, these stigmatized elements also help to symbolize a traditional Settler lifestyle. The Settler lifestyle of trapping came about through a hybridization of Indian, European and Inuit cultural traits. It is this quality of shared cultural traits which simultaneously threatens and bolsters Settler ethnic identity. This is because Settler ethnic identity is established in relation to the ethnic identity of Indians, who are the closest neighbours of North West River Settlers, and so Settler identity must be seen as significantly different from that of the Indians.

North West River Settlers do not construct their ethnic identity in relation to the Inuit, and so the latter do not pose a threat to the management of Settler ethnic identity. As Kennedy (1982:106-7) has pointed out, the Settlers in other coastal Labrador communities, which are shared with Inuit, find it easier to co-opt Indians as friends while maintaining social distance from the Inuit of their own communities, and I suggest that it is because these Settlers are constructing their ethnic identities in relation to the Inuit.

In this chapter we have investigated the relationship between occupation, status, and social characters in North West River society, and have found that occupational differences, which represent relative social status in the community, have been translated into different social characters. Now let us explore the means by which social characters can be manipulated in a conversation where participants express their ethnic identity in relation to Indians in different ways.

Portfolio Two: 1930s to Present

Photograph A: The River Crossing circa 1930. In 1960 a cable car was installed. It ran using crews from both the north and south banks until the bridge was comple - ted in 1980.

Photograph B: The bridge under construction in 1979. The canoe ferry and the cable car required co-operation between the inhabitants of the north and south banks of the community. Once the bridge was in use, there was no need for such co-opera - tion.

Photograph C: A home in Upalong.

Photograph D: Gardens on the Beach.

Photograph E: Uncle Harvey Montague.

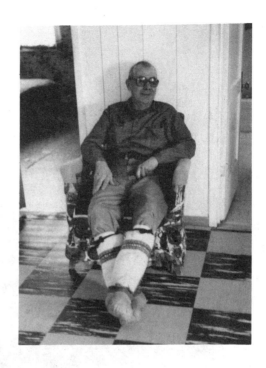

Photograph F: Ross Baikie.

Photograph G: Stewart Baikie.

Photograph H: Uncle Johnny Michelin with his daughter, Joyce. Johnny Michelin is a trapper and prospector. He acted as a guide for the Churchill Falls Development (see Chapter 2, Footnote 24).

Photograph I: Out for some trout…

Photograph J: …and a partridge or two.

Photograph K: Aunt Edna Campbell with the author.

Leemos! 8

*Social Characters and Social Interaction
in North West River*

My intention in this chapter is to analyse a conversation among seven people in North West River, three of whom are major participants in the conversation and four of whom are peripheral. Through the analysis I wish to draw attention to several things. The social environment in present-day North West River creates an ambience in which different social characters come into existence in response to the demands of other social characters in different situations. In the course of the conversation, the three main participants each espouse several separate and contrasting social characters. Each social character comes into being in the context of the group and through the sides taken and issues raised in the conversation. The different perceptions of Indians thus expressed show the fragmented ethnicity in the social lives of the participants. Perceptions or clichés about Indians are taken up by the participants in response to the requirements of the social situation, and are manipulated in order to define and redefine ethnic differences between the Settlers and Indians.

Among the social characters taken up at different times by different participants in the conversation are 'Settler,' 'trapper,' 'oldtimer,' 'Upalonger,' 'Downalonger,' 'newcomer,' 'outsider' and 'elite.' Other social characters occur in other situations, but the conversation here is typical of those held among the individuals represented, and typical of the social characters they espouse in this particular setting.

Two topical threads run through the conversation, and three debates form around these topics, unfolding in an 'ABA' arrangement as the discussion among the participants progresses. Each debate changes the parameters of the conversation, and the participants espouse different social characters as the relationship between the social characters changes. Influences of past economic activities become apparent in the perceptions espoused in the conversation, the most noticeable being that of trapping. The three debates focus in contrasting ways upon the boundary drawn between Settlers and Indians. One of the focal issues concerns land claims, in which Indian claims exclude the Settlers and therefore put them in opposition to the Indians. In the first debate, the Settlers perceive themselves to be disenfranchised by Indian land claims. The other issue, differences between Settler and Indian land use and harvesting practices, is taken up in the second debate. In this debate, Settlers define themselves in relation to Indians by using differences in land use and lifestyle, and in this case, Indians are needed as a 'sounding board' for Settler identity. In the final debate, the participants return to their position as opponents of the Indians through their opposition to the Indians' land claims, but in doing so, they draw upon their Inuit heritage, an allegiance which they consider gives them claim to native status, and through this, added claim to Labrador as their home (or territory).

The conversation takes place in the home of two of the participants. It is a weekday and the participants are drinking beer. I had asked to interview one of the hosts and had been invited to join them for a drink and carry out my interview at the same time; hence, I am one of the peripheral participants. The extract used below comes from the later part of the evening, after several beers have been consumed and spirits are high. By this time, too, the participants are less aware of the more formal aspects of the interview. The members of the group are all known to each other, and have various connections to the community of North West River. Of the three main participants, Jones is a relative newcomer to the community, and Toby and Frank are from long-established North West River families. Of the peripheral participants, Alec and Mary are related to Toby, and Sam is friend and workmate of Jones and Toby. I am present as researcher.

Toby, the host, in his late thirties, is a Downalonger from a family which has been in the region for nearly two hundred years. His forebear had been a 'planter' and independent trader in Hamilton Inlet. His great-grandfather and grandfather had been trappers and his father a local entrepreneur. Toby works as a linesman for the province's telephone company but also has access to traplines and cabins along the Crooked River which he makes use of on weekends and holidays. He shares these facilities with other family members. His wife and cousin are both present as minor participants; his cousin, Alec, often echoing the sentiments of the other speakers. Alec is one of the local wildlife wardens, and as such is occasionally asked for information about animal populations and the environment.

Frank, in his early forties, is also from a longstanding North West River family but, unlike Toby, he is an Upalonger. His forebear came out from Orkney just over a hundred years ago to work with the Hudson's Bay Company and was one of the first men to settle in North West River, on the Upalong bank. His great-grandfather and grandfather were trappers with the Hudson's Bay Company, and his father still traps. Frank works full-time at the steam plant on the Goose Bay Airbase, but also spends much of his spare time and his planned holidays trapping with his brother and father. As such, he can be said to have two occupations: mechanic and trapper. As a bachelor, Frank often forms friendships with the incoming staff of the International Grenfell Association and other outsiders. He also has an interest in the history of the region and collects old books about Labrador by various scientists and adventurers who have passed through the region in the preceding hundred years. This hobby is both fed by, and gives access to, the outsider elite which is forming in the community. He and Toby grew up together in North West River and are close friends.

Jones is in his late twenties. He grew up in North West River after his father moved to the region as a construction worker; thus he does not have the connections to North West River that Frank and Toby do, nor does he have 'trapper' or 'oldtimer' status. He works as a linesman with Toby and with Sam, a minor participant in the conversation. Sam is from a North West River family but he now lives in Happy Valley-Goose Bay and is paying a social call.

Jones: Who's claiming the land? I mean, nobody owns the land!

Sam: They [the Indians] only moved there! Jesus!

Jones: Whether it's white people or Indians, I don't think anybody owns the land. Land is land! I mean, whoever travels and uses it, eh?

(Assent from the group)

Jones: But the fact is, I don't think anyone should cut in on somebody's territory who's been using [the land] there for such extent of time.

Toby: They didn't used to stay in one place. They were moving all over the frigging country, right? They can't go claiming something just because they've moved back to North West River—because they're settled here now! Because they were all over the place before. Spread out, see?

Jones: They were nomadic. That's the way they were, eh, boy?

Toby: Just because they settled here, why should they try to claim the land round North West River? 'Cause this was only their place for coming to get a piece of grub and sell a bit of fur, and they'd be off back in the country again.

Sam: If they were like they were, years and years ago, and still use the land, maybe I'd see a little bit of it. But not now! Because, Jesus Christ, they're flying in and.... Uh!, Oh Christ, they're not usin' the land!

Jones: They use the land less than the white man does. ...

Sam: ... using the land mostly for a holiday now!

Toby: You talk to the older guys, the real old guys, and they'd only see the Indians perhaps once a year—come and get some supplies, sell a bit of fur, and they were gone again. How can they claim the land round this area?

Evie: Well, they're not. They're claiming inland!

Sam: Yeah! They're claiming half of Labrador!

Jones: But how can they claim inland when there's a lot of Caucasian trappers been out there? Trapping for years and years and generations?

Evie: How many generations have they been there?

Jones: I don't know. Well, I couldn't give you an exact 'mount, but I'd say there's been about ... oh! More than five generations!

Toby: I wouldn't know that one!

Evie: No! You don't span five generations! But, you know, they also flooded the best hunting area, didn't they?

(General assent)

Sam: For so many Indians, but not all the Indians. There were so many unaffected, you see. ...

Frank: That was the Indians' main area—up around Michikamau! That was their. ...

Jones: They also flooded Cowie's land. ...

Sam: That was their main stomping ground. ...

Frank: Yes, well. That was all Indian land. People just went up there and took it, in the nineteen hundreds. There wasn't

a white man up there until nineteen hundred and something.

Sam: The people. ... There was no problem with the Indians until
they went up the 'Height of Land,' and then the trappers
got into the Indians up there, but before that, they never
... they never. ...

Frank: They kept pushing the Indians back and back and back.
And it was in the 1900s before any white man went up
there trapping. Old Uncle Bob, and them. They were the
first ones up there trapping. And Grandfather Mustard,
and Uncle Bert, and three or four more. They were the first.

Evie: What did they find when they went up there?

Frank: Pardon?

Toby: Fur!

Evie: What did they find? That the Indians were hostile?

Frank: Well, eh. They only went up to make a new trapline,
because the people were getting more plentiful and everyone claimed a piece of land, and they would just keep
going, more and more, and ...

Toby: Moving into the country. Yeah.

Frank: ... running out of land! That's all! They had to go further
back.

Toby: To catch the furs, to make a living for the family, right!
There was more people. That's all!

Evie: Yes, but how did this affect the Indians?

Frank: There wasn't a piece of land, maybe for sixty or seventy
miles!

Evie: How would that affect the Indians if they were supposed
to be hunting out there?

Jones: They were still doing the same as they were.

Evie: Still hunting?

Toby: Well! No! T'would affect the Indians somewhat, like Frank
said. The Indians would probably move on to 'nother area.

Frank: Yep. And, like Alec said. They didn't retaliate that much,
they retaliated a little, eh?

Alec: No, uh. ...

Evie: Like what did they do?

Frank: I think they cocked a gun 'n' that, they. ...

Alec: Burned somebody's tilt and that. It wasn't a big lot.

Sam: You're talking of going into Churchill Falls, and on beyond that, eh?

Frank: That was always a main trapping area, though, eh? That's the caribou main area, [the] herd area. ...

Toby: Indians never trapped, see?

Evie: No?

Toby: They never ever trapped! Not proper! They catch a few skins —mink and beaver—and they'd walk down a fox rather than set a trap for it. Hit on a fresh track, and they'd walk 'im down in snowshoes, and they get 'im that way, eh? And then they'd get a few skins and come back in and trade 'un in for supplies and then they'd be gone again.

Evie: They would rather walk a fox down than trap it?

Toby: That's the way they done it!

Frank: And the same way with otters, that's the way they used to hunt otters a lot too. They'd get their feeding places, and know where they were going to be in the evening and that, eh? Like a little bit of water where they would come up and feed 'n' eat. They knew all those places, where the rapids were—under the ice, 'n' where the otter travels across. Otters and beavers 'n' that was their main animals. ...

Toby: Water animals, eh? They never go at cats or foxes—regards with traps, eh? Like a fox! I know! I talked with old Michel Pasteen, and he says they get a fresh track and they walk 'un down, eh? Or run 'im down, or whatever, eh? Then shoot 'un.

Frank: I don't see why Alec didn't run—or walk—that one down the other day, up Grand Lake!

(Laughter)

Toby: That's what he told me, anyway! He's an old guy, he's still living yet, but I mean he used to salmon fish, well, living across the Bay and I was over there salmon fishing. I dunno how old I was. Eighteen, I s'pose, when I used to go up there. I stayed over there myself, camping, and I'd visit them, you know? Michel Pasteen!

Evie: They used to eat beaver meat?

Frank: Oh yes. They'd eat beaver, porcupine and caribou. That's what they nearly lived on, eh?

Jones: There's nothing wrong with beaver!

Frank: And they'd get a few skins of fur and then buy flour and other necessary foods.

Toby: That's what they were doing, eh? Just surviving, eh?

Jones: Living off the land, that's all the Indians used to do.

Evie: They can't do that from North West River, though, can they?

Sam: Well, they never used to live in North West River that long. They'd just come into town to pick up supplies and then go back in the country again, eh? Then they were back in their own country and doing their own thing on their own again, eh?

Frank: That's the difference. ...

Jones: No one can live off the land now, anyway. ...

Evie: Why not?

Toby: There's nobody really lives off the land, but there's white people who live off the land more than the Indians do, eh?

Jones: Because they can't. Can you imagine every person who wanted to go and trap, and hunt? Every man just go out together? I mean, not together but just go out and do it. Nobody would make anything! There's not enough land, I mean. No way! Okay, you've got guys here with traplines. That's good. Nobody's gonna interfere. Here, so far, it's good. Here. On the coast people don't respect traplines any more, but here they do.

Toby: But on the coast, Jones, they never had no big traplines. Nothing like that, either. They were living off of fish, selling cod and that was their main stability.

Jones: Let's put it this way, then! Let's say that everyone went out and trapped. And we had the same line as you did. Okay?

Toby: Okay!

Jones: And everybody went out and trapped like you did. And everybody went out and hunted the same damned thing.

Now, do you think—honest opinion—could you make a living off o' your fucking traps and furs? What you haul in on trapline, could you make a living on that?

Toby: I'd be living up Grand Lake, somewhere by myself in my tilt, to make it through.

Jones: Would you do it, though?

Toby: Would I do it? No! I wouldn't do it, but you probably could.

Jones: Okay. You could, but that's YOU. And you got half of Grand Lake! Now, if everybody wanted to do that...!

Toby: Without a snowmobile...

Jones: Just imagine if everybody wanted to do that. If everybody went up there and tried to do that. It would not be possible! Definitely not be possible! Blue [Toby] could go up there! He could make a living. Sure, he'd survive. But he wouldn't be a rich man. And he wouldn't be as well off as he is now!

Toby: I wouldn't have a snowmobile. ...

Jones: Yeah! He wouldn't be as well off as he is now! Like he said, he wouldn't have a snowmobile.

Toby: Might have a canoe or something for paddling round in the lake!

Jones: There you go, you see! It can't be done!

Toby: Evie, eh. You talked to a lot of Indians, I s'pose, eh?

Evie: Not much, this time!

Toby: Do they think they can live off the land?

Evie: I don't know any more. The last time I spoke to Indians about it was 1977. ...

Toby: What did they think then?

Evie: They thought they could, but I think they've changed their minds. ...

Jones: Well, I don't think they could. I don't think they could then. As far as I'm concerned, right here—Frank and Tobe trapping, and Alec—they're doing as good as anybody else. As good as anybody I know. And Frank, Frank is far ahead of anybody else when it comes to that, eh?

Evie: (to Frank) You reckon you could make a living, trapping?

Frank: Well, if you made a living, you'd have to go back in around the 'Height of Land' or something. Have all your equipment and everything and operate that way. Couple of fellers could make a lot of money.

Jones: To yourself?

Frank: Well, there's a bunch of them in there now—25 to 30 trappers there. ...

Jones: Wouldn't it have to be to yourself. Twenty-five to 30 trappers now, then?

Alec: No! No. Let's see, now. Last year, doing it part-time, you made a half decent wage!

Frank: We made $7,000 in two months last year! And the last year, we made $30,000 doing it part-time! And there's 30 to 40 trappers trapping the same area as we are! Exactly the same! There's 3 or 4 traps in the same area!

Jones: Now, let's say a bunch o' potential trappers would like to go trapping but can't, like myself! I'd like to go trapping— I'd love to trap, but I can't! I don't have nowhere to go, right? You just say, everybody like myself, who had the same feeling as myself, was to go in there. That would cut your territory down. Cut down everybody and next thing you know, you're down to about $1,500 a year and. ...

Frank: I know! I know there's not room for everyone to trap. That's only simple! But it is possible to make a living off of it now, for a certain amount of people. The land can only do so many people; there's only so many skins of fur!

Jones: That's exactly true!

Evie: How many people do you reckon?

Frank: Oh! That's hard to say. ...

Alec: You could never be able to tell. I mean, you could say— there's so many studies done. ...

Toby: And you don't know the price of fur.

Frank: The price of fur might drop. ...

Toby: The price of fur might drop. ... Like I was saying, a man in there with a cabin and a canoe would probably survive for the rest of his life—the price of fur would have to go down an awful lot to affect him. ...

Sam: Like, in there there's mostly marten. Marten and fox. ...

Toby: It's life whether the price of fur goes up or down, eh? It would have to go down an awful lot to affect you if you were just living off the land, eh?

Frank: Like, you may as well say, like the Brauns down here, lives off the land all right!

Alec: Yep! They're the only ones left!

Sam: You take those guys, for example, and that's exactly what they done!

Toby: ...and they don't have snowmobiles. ...

Sam: They don't get a whole lot, either, you know. Trapping in winter and fishing in summer. ...

Jones: As far as I'm concerned, the longer we hold on to this trapline situation, the better it is!

Evie: Why?

Jones: Let's for example say that Tobe Dunn owns a trapline right up to, just above Cape Caribou, on the north and south side. Okay, let's say that I go cut in there, and then somebody else goes cuts in there, and somebody else, and so on. Okay, you're talking about four ways now! You're talking a four-way cut on all the furs! But I think [that] as long as we hold on to the trapline situation [then] there's this person, he's got his trapline. Why should we invade it? Why should anyone invade it? That person has a trapline. It's his trapline through tradition! Not through law or nothing, but through tradition. But it is his. ...

Frank: The Indians owned it first!

Jones: Yeah, okay!

Toby: But do the Indians trap up there, though?

Sam: The Indians used to trap up there. ...

Jones: But they were so nomadic, you didn't know where they were going to be next. ...

Toby: But how can you prove they used to trap in Grand Lake?

Frank: Records say, Hudson's Bay Company records say that they were trapping right round here!

Toby: It does?

Frank: Oh yes.

Sam: But how much did the Indians trap? They only trapped a few water animals!

Frank: 'Twas only a couple of white men setting traps here first. It's only lately that the trapping got going. The white people started breaking off from the Hudson's Bay Company and started trapping—few traps here and there. ...

Toby: Yeah, but! The Indians only ever trapped water animals!

Frank: Yeah. But I mean that they trapped and used the land, and they'd get what they could and that.

Toby: Yeah, well they still do eh?

Frank: Even the old store manager here used to go up and force this feller out and that feller. ...

Jones: You don't believe everything you read, eh?

Frank: Well, the Hudson's Bay Company records are very good and straight!

Jones: Just like their prices and their evaluation of furs! I don't believe in the Hudson's Bay Company!

Evie: Yes, but it is obvious that the Indians were here first! I mean, you can't dispute that they were here first!

Jones: I don't know. I'm not really sure about that. ...

Evie: The Europeans that came here found Indians. ...

Toby: Maybe they were here, but I don't know about in their numbers. ... I mean, you don't know how long they stayed here. ...

Evie: No, but they were here first. ...

Jones: They were nomadic!

Mary: How can you say that the Indians were here first?

Evie: Because the first white men here found Indians, and archaeological sites all over the place date them as being here before white people. I'm not an archaeologist, but there are sites. ...

Toby: Maybe they just passed through here?

Frank: But that's mostly what they did! They passed through everywhere, eh? They usually followed the caribou. That's where they were—they stayed round the caribou!

Jones: You can't expect them to come in and dirty some place up and then come back and try to claim it!

Sam: I don't think they should get anything from their land claims!

Jones: I don't, either!

Mary: Even if they were here first, I mean, God! We all got to live somewhere!

Jones: They come through and dirt this place up!

Sam: It would be all right if they were living the way they used to, but not the way they're living now! They don't deserve it!

Jones: They dirtied this place up. ...

Evie: They dirtied it up?

Jones: The Indians came through. They lived in this place until it got so bloody dirty that they moved on to the next. That's why they're nomadic, as far as I'm concerned! And I talked to a few older people and they told me — 'Well, this is where I came from.' They told me that they stayed in one place until it got so dirty that they just moved on.

Toby: You think they should get money, Evie?

Jones: I don't think they should get any money ...!

Evie: I'm asking you guys. You live here, I don't!

Jones: But, there's a thing ... you've got to think of another thing! Whether it's using the land or abusing the land.

Sam: If they were still using it, then I could see ...

Frank: It's changing all the time, between the Indians. You can see it. Used to be a time when everyone ... oh, it's changed an awful lot. You can see it changing all the time. Even when we were little fellers. Used to know all the Indians by name and everything one time. Now I hardly know any of them.

Sam: Because there's so many!

Toby: Now they want to claim the whole of Labrador!

Alec: They've only just moved in in the last couple of years!

Jones: Yes, but what happens to us lot in the middle?

Mary: We came from the Eskimos for God's sake!

Evie: You should be Metis. ...

Frank: Everyone is Metis here. ...

Jones: That's what I put on my job application form — Registered Metis!

Toby: Jeese! I got Eskimo blood in me all over the place! We're half 'limeys' and half 'skeemos!'

Jones: S'true, yeah ... 'leemos!'

(Laughter)

Following the conversation through the contribution of any one participant produces an often chaotic and contradictory set of arguments. However, if the participants are seen as contributing fragments of conversation which embody perceptions from several different but overlapping social characters, then the conversation gains an interesting form of coherence.

The continuum most noticeable at work in this conversation is that of the 'oldtimer' versus the 'newcomer.' 'Oldtimers'' roots in the community can go back to the pioneer settlement of the region, in some cases as much as two hundred years, but more commonly back to the early days of the fur trade in the mid-nineteenth century. Many of the oldtimers were trappers and because the fur trade shaped a significant part of the community's past, the trapping way of life seems particularly representative of Settler culture. The 'trapper' social character is based upon the experiences of the older trappers towards the end of the fur trade in Labrador. Both characters share elements of a more general Settler identity; hence, 'oldtimers' and 'trappers' can be seen to overlap but not necessarily coincide. The term 'Settler' becomes an umbrella term which is used by older Settlers as well as non-Settlers for both 'oldtimer' and 'trapper.' It refers to those born in Labrador with some Inuit ancestry, although the term 'Labradorian' is used more frequently nowadays by Settlers when referring to themselves.[1] The term 'Labradorian,' however, has interesting connotations, since it was initiated by politically active community members who aimed to consolidate Settler identity for political reasons, and it does not necessarily indicate Inuit ancestry. Rather, the term implies an identity based upon place of residence, and it is therefore used by newcomers and certain outsiders as well as by Settlers. These characters — 'trapper,' 'oldtimer,' and 'Settler' — are placed in contrast to 'newcomers,' 'outsiders' and (admittedly, for rather different reasons) the 'elite' who also form part of the community. Although individuals are tied to particular sets of social characters in the context of the conversation, they are still capable of swinging between social characters, and they thereby maintain a fluid social identity.

Since social characters operate in juxtaposition to each other, the espousal of a social character and the concomitant range of perceptions by one participant draws other participants into the espousal of complementary or contradictory characters and perceptions. This can be seen in the conversation above, when Toby and Frank become Downalonger and Upalonger in relation to each other. The social characters represented in this conversation also display a 'nested,' or recursive interrelationship: Labradorians can be Settlers, Settlers can be oldtimers, and oldtimers can be Upalongers (but need not be). Each of these overlapping characters, growing out of each other, is marked by changing perceptions.

The three main participants espouse a number of social characters which draw upon a reservoir of perceptions both complementary and contrastive. Jones is a newcomer who wants to be part of the Settler community. Throughout the conversation he swings between the social characters of newcomer, Settler and Labradorian, alternately drawing the others into social characters in opposition to him — as Settlers versus outsiders, as oldtimers versus newcomers and as trappers versus non-trappers — and then as allies when he acts as a Settler in opposition to Indians, and as a disenfranchised Labradorian middleman versus other ethnic groups.

As an aspiring Settler, he begins the debate on land claims with a series of statements which co-opt the other Settlers into expressing resentment towards Indian land claims:

Jones: Who's claiming the land? I mean nobody owns the land! Whether it's white people or Indians, I don't think anybody owns the land. Land is land! I mean, whoever travels and uses it, eh?

Toby: Just because they settled here, why should they try to claim the land round North West River?

Sam: Oh Christ, they're not using the land!

Later, as 'newcomer,' Jones is excluded from the conversation while Toby and Frank, as 'oldtimers' and 'trappers,' discuss the relative merits and differences between Indian and Settler harvesting practices. He then reintroduces the theme of trapline rights several times, explicitly as an outsider to trapping culture:

Jones: Now, let's say a bunch o' potential trappers would like to go trapping but can't, like myself! I'd like to go trapping— I'd love to trap, but I can't! I don't have nowhere to go, right?

This allows Toby and Frank to expound on the trapping way of life, and show their knowledge and expertise in that area, specifically as trappers and oldtimers in contrast to a newcomer.

In the concluding debate, Jones finds a way of becoming focal in the conversation again, by changing from the social character of 'outsider' to the social character of the disenfranchised 'Labradorian' resident. In this guise he is able to draw the others into agreement with him.

The social characters Toby moves through in the course of the conversation include 'Settler,' 'trapper,' 'oldtimer,' 'Downalonger' and 'Labradorian.' He is at first drawn into Jones's tirade against Indian land claims, but then switches characters to join Frank as an 'oldtimer' and 'trapper,' leaving Jones as the naive 'newcomer' and non-trapper. By discussing harvesting practices, Toby and Frank are able to develop their Settler identity in contrast to Indians. But, *within* this context of 'trappers' and 'oldtimers,' Toby and Frank also become social characters in contrast to each other. Toby is a 'Downalonger.' He doesn't spend much of his time trapping, and tends to romanticize the trapping way of life as an 'oldtimer':

Toby: I wouldn't have a snowmobile...might have a canoe or something for paddling round in the lake!

This is in contrast to Frank, an 'Upalonger,' who traps as a secondary occupation and talks about the logistics of modern day trapping:

Frank: Well, if you made a living, you'd have to go back in around the 'Height of Land' or something. Have all your equipment and everything and operate that way. Couple of fellers could make a lot of money.

As we have seen in Chapter Seven, 'Upalongers' and 'Downalongers' form yet another continuum in North West River social life. Toby, as an 'oldtimer' reminiscing about salmon fishing as a young man, invokes the memory of his friendship with Michel Pasteen, an old Indian. This adds to his social character of 'trapper' and 'oldtimer,' and gives weight to his perceptions of Indians in response to the more detailed information Frank, the 'Upalonger,' offers:

Toby: Indians never trapped, see...they'd walk down a fox rather than set a trap for it. ...

Frank: And the same way with otters, that's the way they used to hunt otters a lot too. They'd get their feeding places, and know where they were going to be in the evening and that, eh? Like a little bit of water where they would come up and feed 'n' eat. They knew all those places, where the rapids were—under the ice, 'n' where the otter travels across. Otters and beavers 'n' that was their main animals. ...

Toby: Water animals, eh? They never go at cats or foxes. ... I know! I talked with old Michel Pasteen. ...

Later in the discussion, Toby leaves his 'oldtimers' dialogue with Frank and again joins Jones, who is reintroducing the trapline rights argument, and he and Jones become 'Settlers' in opposition to Indian land claims:

Jones: ... That person has a trapline. It's his trapline through tradition! Not through law or nothing, but through tradition. But it is his. ...

Frank: The Indians owned it first!

Jones: Yeah, okay!

Toby: But do the Indians trap up there, though ... how can you prove they used to trap in Grand Lake?

Frank: Records say, Hudson's Bay Company records say that they were trapping right round here!

Toby: It does?. ... Yeah, but! ...

Finally, Toby teases Jones about his espousal of Metis identity, and they are both able to joke about their 'middle-men' situation in the politics of ethnicity.

Frank is the last of the main participants to join the conversation, and begins by offering some historical information about Indian land use before the Settler trapping era got underway. His espoused social character of 'outsider-elite,' with the concomitant perceptions of an historian in support of Indians is, in part, in response to my presence. It also reflects his interest in the history of the community and his friendship, through this interest, with the outsider-newcomer elite forming in the community.

He is soon drawn into conversation with Toby, however, in the character of 'oldtimer' with knowledge of Indian harvesting patterns. During this part of the conversation, Frank, in responding to Toby, reinforces their common identity as longstanding residents of North West River who experience an affinity with Indians. He and Toby both do this by displaying an understanding and appreciation of the differences between Indian and Settler harvesting patterns.

A little later on Frank is drawn back into the conversation by Jones, who this time attributes to him the 'Upalonger' social character of a relatively successful present-day trapper:

Jones: ...As far as I'm concerned, right here—Frank and Tobe trapping, and Alec—they're doing as good as anybody else. As good as anybody I know. And Frank, Frank is far ahead of anybody else when it comes to that, eh?

At first, he espouses the social character of the experienced Upalong trapper and is able to provide the others with accurate information about trapping conditions above the 'Height of Land,' where he traps. But he then uses the example of some well-known and respected old Downalongers who, in his opinion, actually live off the land as full-time trappers in contrast to himself, a part-time trapper. Frank's use of the 'Downalongers' as an example of Settlers who trap is in contradiction to his 'Upalonger' social character, since 'Upalongers' are supposed to possess greater bush skills than are 'Downalongers.' It illustrates Frank's ambivalence towards being the 'Upalonger.' On the one hand, he uses the character to augment his Settler trapper identity, while on the other hand, he backs away from his identification with it.

In response to Jones' reintroduction of the trapline debate, Frank switches back to his character of the 'elite' historian. He states that the land belonged to the Indians before Settlers took it over for trapping, and he again offers information on land use, this time from a source (the Hudson's Bay Company records) which he has appreciated through his association with the incoming elite. This source of information is not readily recognized by the other participants, since it has currency in social situations to which they are seldom party. Later, in order to gain ground again as a Settler, Frank vehemently supports his fellow participants by agreeing with their analysis of Indians as nomadic, which lessens, in Settlers' eyes, their claim to the land around North West River.

Having established that there are a number of social characters at play throughout the conversation, I wish to examine what the fragmentary nature of social interaction in North West River society has to say about ethnicity in the community.

The changes in conversational content and social characters cause significant changes in the participants' perceptions of Indians and Indian/Settler relations. As modern 'Settlers,' North West River inhabitants perceive the now-resident Indians as constituting a threat to the Settlers' access to land around the community:

Jones: Who's claiming the land? I mean, nobody owns the land!

Toby: They didn't used to stay in one place. ... They can't go claiming something just because they've moved back to North West River. ...

Sam: If they were like they were, years and years ago, and still using the land, maybe I'd see a little bit of it. But not now!

Jones: They use the land less than the white man does. ...

Sam: Yeah! They're claiming half of Labrador!

Jones: But how can they claim inland when there's a lot of Caucasian trappers been out there? Trapping for years and years and generations?

In these fragments of the conversation, the participants accept 'white man' and 'Caucasian' identity in contrast to the Indians. And yet, they use the same argument that Indians use in making land claims—that of long-term residence and of the importance of the environment as an integral part and expression of their culture.

As 'oldtimers' and 'trappers,' North West River inhabitants use Indians in several ways to support Settler identity:

Toby: Indians never trapped, see ... not proper ... they'd walk [the animal] down in snowshoes, and they get 'im that way, eh?

Frank: And the same way with otters, that's the way they used to hunt otters a lot too. ... I don't see why Alec didn't run—or walk—that one down the other day, up Grand Lake!

Toby uses his friendship with Michel Pasteen to give weight to his argument about Indian/Settler harvesting differences. The Indian 'Michel Pasteen' is different to those Indians criticized earlier for claiming land. In this case Toby finds it socially useful to claim personal knowledge of 'Indians,' whereas to claim friendship during the debate about land use and land claims was inappropriate. In calling upon an old friendship, or knowledge of Indians, Toby is stressing his 'oldtimer' Settler identity by showing how different, within a narrow range of land users and occupiers, Settlers are from Indians. Hence, 'Indians' become a resource for Settler identity maintenance. Similarly, Frank is able to joke about the differences between Indian and Settler practices when he 'wonders' why Alec was unable to catch himself a fox by simply spotting the animal's tracks. In both cases, Indians are seen as complementary to Settlers, and, in fact, are needed in order to form Settler identity.

More subtly, Toby, the Downalonger, and Frank, the Upalonger, perceive Indians differently. Frank uses his Upalonger knowledge of Indian practices — details of their hunting methods and explanations of how and why they hunt that way — whereas Toby uses an historically distant perception of Indians as bush companions, a perception which has grown out of a romanticizing of trapping as a way of life. From Frank's point of view, Indians display a logic towards their environment and occupation which he, as a practising trapper, is able to appreciate. For Toby, the 'Indian' becomes part and parcel of a way of life which he does not practise, but which has nevertheless shaped part of his identity.

In the final debate, the conversation focuses upon yet another twist in Settlers' manipulation of identity. The distinction between Inuit and Indian is well known to the Settlers, and they are able to side with the Inuit when Indian land claims distance them from any affiliation with Indians. In fact, their recognition of the ethnic distinction between Indians and Inuit creates an anomaly which enables them to juggle the two sides of their identity — as a group with some claim to nativeness through part Inuit ancestry, with a distinct culture, and as a group in opposition to the Indians with whom they share a similar adaptation and environment. This use of the situation, I suggest, can be maintained only while there is sufficient actual distance between Settlers and Inuit.[2] In other contexts, both Indians and Inuit are comfortably joined together in Settler perceptions.

Through their perceptions of Indians, Settlers' perceptions of themselves fluctuate — from 'native Labradorian Settlers' (a threatened minority), to secure white Canadians with a sense of history and destiny. Because of their particular situation in the Canadian arctic, as middlemen between indigenous native minorities and mainstream European Canadians, North West River Settlers can afford, or even need to have, a fluid ethnic identity. For them, ethnicity does not exist outside any particular social situation. No social character is more 'real' than another, and no ethnic identity is more 'true' to Settler identity than the one that emerges in any particular social context. Depending upon the social situation and the economic climate in which they find themselves, Settlers draw upon aspects of their identity and relationship with Indians as a resource, as a social expedient, and, indeed, as a 'native' game.

Conclusion   9

In this book, I have argued that Settler ethnic identity is entwined
with perceptions of Indian ethnic identity. Settler perceptions of
Indians reveal the differences by which Settlers define themselves
as Settlers. This approach rests upon the understanding that,
firstly, the important criterion in ethnic identity is the *defining* of
differences between groups, and not necessarily the *content* of those
differences; and, secondly, that the difference in identities between
groups is most apparent when groups are in juxtaposition to each
other.

The Settlers of North West River use cultural adaptations, which
they have acquired over a period of 200 years, in their creation and
management of a Settler ethnic identity in juxtaposition to Indians.
For the outside world, Settlers are the colonists of lands which do
not belong to them as a special social group. Neither their language
nor their religious practices separate them from mainstream Canadian life. In fact, they rest their claim to ethnic uniqueness, and
thus, identity, upon a short-lived cultural hybridization which gave
rise to a distinctive lifestyle. And yet, we have seen that they are able
to create and maintain an ethnic identity by referring to the differences that they perceive between themselves and another group
which has defined itself 'legitimately' (in the eyes of the Provincial
and Federal Governments) as an ethnic group.

The hybrid nature of Settler ethnic identity is complicated by the
fact that it is, in part, the acculturation of Indian cultural traits,
while, at the same time, it defines itself in opposition to Indian ethnic
identity. The contradiction in Settler ethnic identity is shown in the
relationship between the social characters of 'Upalonger' and 'Downalonger' which is explored in Chapter Seven. The social character of
'Upalonger' forms an ethnic identity within the broader Settler
ethnic identity because other Settlers see 'Upalongers' as sharing

cultural traits with Indians. On the one hand, these shared traits are expressive of Settler identity, and on the other hand, they threaten its integrity as a distinct identity.

In his work on ethnic groups and boundaries, Barth (1969) postulates that ethnic interaction is much more noticeable and definable when it takes place at the perimeters of the group than within the group. In other words, maintenance of group identity requires the maintenance of a boundary between that group and other such groups, and it is often the case that such perimeters become accentuated when one group is in proximity to another.

In North West River, sedentarization — of the Settlers since 1944 and of the Indians in 1961 — has meant that Settlers and Indians are now in year-round proximity to each other, and, as can be seen from Chapter Six, this proximity has caused a change in Settler perceptions of Indians. Since sedentarization, there has been a substantial rise in the ethnic and political consciousness of both groups. The Naskapi/Montagnais Innu Association (NMIA) was formed in 1975 and the Settlers are in the process of forming a Metis Association. Thus ethnicity is the social and political outcome of diverse, and often conflicting, historical experience.

At the beginning of this book, I made the point that changing social environments cause the fragmentation of social identity. The development of social characters illustrates the fragmentation of Settler identity in three ways. Firstly, social characters develop in response to past experiences of certain Settlers, and they are, in turn, used to express contemporary identities. Secondly, because social characters emerge in response to the particular past experiences of certain Settlers, they cannot represent the experience of every Settler. Therefore, some social characters are less manipulable than others, and limit the fluidity of certain Settlers' identities. And, thirdly, the fragmentation of social experience is also reflected in the recursive nature of social characters.

Each of the later chapters, while exploring the formation of social characters in the community, also brings to light a theoretical complication in the development of the idea of social characters. Chapter Five follows the evolution of the social character of 'trapper' from the economic activity of trapping and the reality of the trapping lifestyle. It is difficult to isolate the point at which the social character emerges from the economic reality of trapping because the ingredients of the social character of trapper are drawn from the past experiences of the Settlers who pursued trapping as a career. Moreover, the trappers are themselves embedded in the idea of the 'trapper,' which no longer exists as an economic role, and so they are also espousing the social character that they have helped to create through their own reminiscences.

Chapter Six shows that social characters are espoused by those who have not directly experienced trapping as a way of life. As soon as the idea of the 'trapper' is taken up by community members as a valid expression of social identity, then the social character is created out of the historical reality. Also, once it is removed from its historical context and becomes a social expedient, the development and progress of the social character is no longer in the control of the Settlers who have provided the ingredients of the character through their experiences. The traits are selected as much by those using the social character as by those who provide the ingredients. The extent to which the social character of 'trapper' is espousable by non-trappers bears directly upon the problem posed in Chapter Seven.

Chapter Seven reveals the extent to which social characters are not freely exchangeable between individuals. The social characters of "Upalonger" and "Downalonger" are limited in their applicability in that they are not appropriate social characters for all Settlers. "Upalongers" cannot become "Downalongers," nor can "Downalongers" become "Upalongers"; the idea of social character includes the possibility of certain social characters being non-exchangeable. Certain social characters have the quality of limited accessibility because they evolve from experiences which are unevenly distributed throughout the Settler population. If the traits expressed through a social character were universally shared, then there would be no function for the social character, and it would not evolve as something to be espoused. And because social characters, at their moment of separation from historical reality, slip from the control of those whose experiences they express, they can take on negative, as well as positive, attributes.

The final problem, which is related to the questions posed above, and which comes to light in Chapter Eight, is that social characters proliferate. Within the fragmented historical experiences of the community of North West River lies the possibility that multiple social characters may be created, and these are not necessarily separate from each other. In fact, many of the social characters are recursive, with smaller, or lesser, social characters evolving out of the larger coalitions of experiences represented by other social characters, much like a set of Russian dolls. For instance, 'Settler' can be considered to be the generic social character of the North West River population, out of which all other social characters flow. Thus, 'Labradorians' can be 'Settlers,' 'Settlers' can be 'trappers,' and 'trappers' can be 'oldtimers.' At each level, the social character has distinguishing characteristics, but, at the same time, it cannot exist separately from other social characters. Thus, 'Settlers' can be oldtimers, but an 'oldtimer' *is* a 'Settler.' For the same reason, it is difficult to analyse the boundaries between individual social characters, since social characters often spill over into one another, and are often espoused in tandem. So far, social characters have displayed the extent to which Settler identity has become fragmented by the changes that Settlers have experienced in the past, are experiencing now, and will continue to experience in the future. However, in developing the idea of social characters, certain problems have been posed, and these remain unsolved.

Finally, given the fragmented nature of social identity, I suggested that ethnicity becomes a resource to be manipulated. As can be seen in Chapter Eight, Settlers use their perceptions of Indians to create and manipulate Settler identities in order to strengthen and define their perceptions of themselves. Thus, Toby finds an old Indian friend that he can refer to in his conversation about trapping, and this perception of Indians as fellow woodsmen builds upon Toby's self-image as a 'trapper' and 'oldtimer.' But, equally, Indians can be perceived as a threat to Settler identity, as in Jones' and Toby's discussion of Indian land claims. Ethnicity, then, becomes a resource and an impetus for Settlers in the management of their own identity, both among themselves and in a wider context.

Ethnic identity emerges as a political and social resource because it occurs in reference to another ethnic group. From within the morass of possible identities, North West River Settlers have to construct and maintain a distinctive ethnic identity. For them, the 'native game' involves retaining sufficient distinctiveness to maintain individual and communal identity but also expressing enough affiliation with Indians to qualify for some kind of native status in the eyes of the outside world.

Notes

Preface

1. Lydia Campbell is a significant figure in Labrador social history. She was born in Hamilton Inlet in 1818 of an English father and Inuit mother, and the diary she kept represents a rare surviving portrayal of Settler life in nineteenth century Labrador. Her part in the history of North West River is described in Chapter Four.

2. Settlers are the European inhabitants of Scottish, English and French origin, who came to Labrador and married Inuit and, occasionally, Indians during the colonization of eastern Canada.

3. Nowadays, a majority of people from North West River commute to jobs in Happy Valley-Goose Bay. Employment in the community is discussed further in Chapters Two, Six and Seven.

4. Both salmon and cod fishing—subsistence activities for most—are also commercial activities for a number of Labradorians. Other wage-earning summer employment includes fire-fighting, wildlife monitoring, and construction work.

5. I described my project as follows:

   My interest lies in the development of relations between the people of North West River and the people of Sheshatshiu, and in what people think about the relationship between themselves and the Montagnais Indians. I am particularly interested in finding out whether this relationship changes with time, and what causes the change. To do this, I am asking people about the old days, about stories and incidents which happened in the past, whether they remember their dealings with the Indians, and what these were like. I am also finding out about the things which make the two communities different today, and how people feel about these differences (Newsletter of the Town Council of North West River, December 2, 1983).

6. I thank those very gracious women for their friendship and tolerance.

Chapter 1

1. The community of Mud Lake was the regional centre at this time. North West River became the regional centre after Dickie's Lumber Company (based in Mud Lake) had left the region in 1911–12, and when the International Grenfell Association moved its first year-round hospital from Mud Lake to North West River in 1916. See Chapter 2.

2. Renewed interest in the facilities at Goose Bay Airbase is relatively recent—beginning minimally in 1979. At the time of my fieldwork, it had not had any significant effect on the community of North West River.

3. The three are the Labrador Inuit Association, the Newfoundland Federation of Indians and the Naskapi/Montagnais Innu Association.

4. Full membership in the LIA is selected on the basis of genealogical information and by place of birth. People born in North West River are not automatically full members, but can become so if they, or a parent or grandparent, were born east of Mulligan before 1940. People born in Nain, Hopedale, Makkovik, Postville and Rigolet are full members if they, or their parents, were born in one of these communities before 1940. Children of parents from these communities are automatically members, regardless of where they were born. Anyone can become an associate member of the LIA, but this does not confer voting rights nor inclusion in land claims negotiations. The LIA is presently (1987) claiming land north and east of Mulligan (personal communication; Sam Anderson, 1987).

5. North West River is not included in the Canada/Native Peoples of Labrador Agreement. The agreement began with Confederation in 1949 and was amended in 1954, 1965 1972 and 1981. It initially included Nain, Hopedale, Makkovik, Postville, Davis Inlet and what is now Sheshatshit. Rigolet, Black Tickle and Mud Lake were later added but, although it was discussed at various times, North West River has never been included.

6. Zimmerly's book traces the Settlers' transition from a subsistence economy to a wage labour economy made during the twentieth century, using Julian Steward's theory of culture change.

7. "Black box" is the term given to certain formulae used in statistics where numbers are processed through equations but the workings of the equations are not explained, and are not deemed relevant to the final outcome. The term is similarly used in engineering and electronics: "…black boxes: things you don't look inside of. Thus it is often useful to consider only the 'opaque surface' of a component…, while taking its inner workings…for granted" (Haugeland 1985:80). For information on Labrador Indians, I refer the reader to Speck (1935 and 1942), Leacock (1954, 1955 and 1969), McGee (1961), Henriksen (1973), Cooke (1979), Tanner (1977) and Mailhot (1986a and b, and 1988). Jose Mailhot is presently concluding a study of the internal social structure of the Innu community of Sheshatshit.

8. See the publications of the Rhodes-Livingstone Institute at Lusaka, now the Institute for African Studies at the University of Zambia.
9. Lithman (1978) and Braroe (1975) deal directly with the Indian perspective when analysing responses to interaction in Indian/white relations. Inglis (1970) and Carstens (1971) examine the effects of government policies on Indian life and the responses of Indians to government agencies. In all cases, the treatment of whites as groups or individuals is peripheral.
10. Pontings and Gibbins (1976) find very general trends in white Canadian attitudes, but do not analyse perspectives held by a single white group.
11. Barth (1969); Ben-Dor (1961); Brantenberg (1977); Eidheim (1971); Cohen (1974); and Kennedy (1982).

Chapter 2

1. The exact meaning of the term 'planter' is disputed. Some accept it to mean the men who populated the fishing stations in winter, whereas other assume it refers to the owners of the stations. However, planter is the term used in documents quoted in Gosling to describe the men who over-wintered on the coast (see Gosling, 1910).
2. Those in search of opportunities, particularly economic opportunity. See Matthews 1968a and b.
3. Copies of the ledgers and papers of both companies are kept in the Provincial Archives.
4. Matthews (1968b) notes that those merchants who were among the first to enter the fishery were, almost exclusively, those who remained at the end. These long established and comparatively stable family businesses had also become closely related by intermarriage, as well as sharing a common geographical base in the Old World.
5. Possibly such names as Davis, or Davies, and Williams came out at this time.
6. For example, Mesher comes from Mercier or Messier, a Channel Islands name probably from St. Hellier, where vessels called regularly.
7. Among these would most probably be the Blakes, Rumbolts, Sheppards, and Groves.
8. There are a few comprehensive histories of Orkney: Bailey (1971), Linklater (1965) and Shearer et al. (1967) all cover recent history comprehensively, but without depth. Ernest Marwick's unpublished 'Journey From Serfdom' gives a more detailed account. However, I have drawn mainly upon the work of W. P. Thomson (1981 and 1983) which singles out and concentrates on two specific periods and issues in Orcadian history: the enclosure of, and struggle for crofters' rights on one estate in Rousay; and the kelp industry. *The Statistical Account of Orkney 1795-1798, or the Old Statistical Account*, (Sinclair 1927) is a compilation of writings done by the various ministers of the Orkney parishes, and gives descriptions of the life of ordinary Orcadians around the turn of the eighteenth century. *The New Statistical Account*

of Scotland (1845) does the same for the mid-nineteenth century, at the time when recruitment was taking place for the Labrador posts.

9. McGrath's papers are kept in the Provincial Archives of Newfoundland and Labrador in St. John's. Besides copies of the Hudson's Bay Company Journals for the Labrador posts, the papers also include a number of letters, affidavits and other documents to which I refer.

10. Gentlemen were either traders or factors. Traders were in charge of one or two neighbouring posts, whereas factors were in charge of districts with several posts, which were individually run by the traders.

11. According to Goldring, the Indians in Rupert's Land were especially sensitive to class differences, and often refused to deal with ordinary servants in their trading transactions.

12. The Stromness well is recorded as having supplied water to Captain Cook's vessels in 1780 and Franklin's ships in 1845 in addition to the Hudson's Bay Company ships from 1670 to 1891. The well was sealed in 1932, long after the ships had ceased to visit Stromness for either men or water.

13. Nicks has calculated that it cost between £40 and £60 to buy a smallholding (with the livestock and other expenses) in Orkney at that time, and "tradesmen were able to save more in a shorter period of time than labourers. ..." Labourers from before 1790 and up to 1804 had to work eight years before their savings exceeded £60, whereas tradesmen could save over £65 in their first five years. After 1804, it took labourers four years to save the same £60, whereas tradesmen could put by as much as £100 in the same period (Nicks 1980:121).

14. In 1799 there were 530 men in Canada with the Hudson's Bay Company, four out of five were Orcadians (Shearer et al. 1967:64). In 1800, approximately 390 out of 498 men employed by the Hudson's Bay Company were from Orkney (Nicks 1980:102). An estimated 2,000 men were employed by Hudson's Bay Company around 1821, before the amalgamation of the Hudson's Bay Company with the North West Company (Goldring 1980:12) by which time less than 40 per cent were Orcadian (Nicks 1980:102).

15. I have used two complementary studies for the following information. Nicks' study covers the period between 1790 and 1821, which is before amalgamation, and concentrates on the recruitment of Orkneymen from the parish of Orphir. Goldring's study covers the period between 1821 and 1900, which is after amalgamation, and deals with recruitment for Rupert's Land.

16. A large proportion of the recruits were the eldest surviving sons in a family; however, younger brothers were often recruited several years after their brothers had signed up.

17. The term 'Canadian,' when used in Hudson's Bay Company historical documents, usually refers to French-speaking 'coureurs de bois,' who were recruited in Lower Canada. The Canadians filled the role of voyagers, coureurs de bois—the canoeists on the inland voyages made in order to transport goods and men between posts.

18. Nicks describes three types of recruit: short-stay of 8–9 years, long-stay of 15 years, and career employees who stayed for 27–29 years on average. Most workers stayed for eight or nine years, which is between one and two contract periods. However, this pattern was established before amalgamation, and may well have been different after 1821.

19. The 'King's Posts' are all communities along the North Shore of Quebec which were once Hudson's Bay Company trading posts. Their origins, however, lie with the French Regime. They comprise: Natashquan; Musquaro; St. Augustine; Mingan and Seven Islands. These posts were sometimes collectively referred to as the 'King's Posts.'

20. The list of names of employees at the North West River post for 1836, recorded in the Hudson's Bay Company journal for that year, are as follows: James Brownley, John Clouston, William Craigie, James Delday, Bazile Dulic, James Jr. and Ignace McKay, Isaac and Gaspard Martin, George, Charles and Alexander McKenzie, Simon Jr. McGillivray, Jean Nolin, Henri and William Pinet, William Sinclair, William Sullivan, Benjamin St. George, Charles Tranquil, and John Voy. There are more than twelve men listed, and more than four of the names could be classified as Orcadian. William and Henri Pinet were mentioned by McGillivray as being Settlers who were hired by the Company (probably as common labourers) from the region of Rigolet.

21. Thomas Bird's business, established by Joseph (presumably his father) in 1810, was based in Forteau, where he was one of the major traders for the cod fishery. Groves, likewise, probably intended to commit his efforts full-time to the fishery. These men were more interested in the fishery than the fur trade, and had possibly extended their activities to Hamilton Inlet for a few seasons in order to try salmon fishing.

22. A tierce is a former liquid measurement, equivalent to 42 (American) wine gallons — or a cask holding this amount.

23. Malcolm Maclean was involved in a dispute with the Hudson's Bay Company over fishing rights at Kenimish sometime during the 1880s, in which the Company wanted to bar him from netting the river. As he was an independent Settler by that time, who was supplied by the Hudson's Bay Company in return for part of his catch, the Company had no grounds on which to prevent him from fishing at the post. He retained his right to fish at Kenimish, where the McLean family still fishes today.

24. Elliot Merrick accompanied a group of North West River trappers up the Hamilton River to their traplines and spent the season trapping with John Michelin in the 'Height of Land.' His adventures are recounted in his book *True North* (1933). The Finnish geographer, Vaino Tanner, carried out a geographical survey of the Labrador peninsula in 1937, and completed an extensive two-volume account of Labrador's customs and geography in 1944. In 1951, Merrick's companion, John Michelin, was a member of another expedition into the Labrador interior, accompanying another Settler, John's cousin Leslie Michelin, and two journalists for the *National Geographic Magazine*. The aim of

this expedition was to photograph the journey to Churchill Falls, which the men made in aluminum canoes over white water rapids, for the magazine (1951).

25. There are numerous sources of information about the International Grenfell Association, both from the point of view of the activities it undertook, and from that of the people who undertook these activities. Grenfell himself was a copious writer, and I have used his auto-biographies to provide an insight into Grenfell's personality and the concerns which led him to establish a branch of the Royal Mission to the Deep Sea Fishermen in Labrador (Grenfell 1919;1932). J. Lennox Kerr's biography (1959) gives details of Grenfell's life from a different perspective, and the operations of the IGA have been selectively documented in the Mission's journal, *Among the Deep Sea Fishers*. Other sources which have been used here include; Kennedy 1985, Moores 1985, and my own experiences as a voluntary worker for the IGA in 1974–75 and 1976–77 also furnish some of the insights.

26. The Mokami Development Association is now the Mokami Regional Development Association (MRDA). It has recently helped to form the Mokami Project Group, the main concern of which is the promotion of Goose Bay Airbase as the location for military expansion — specifically as the location for a future NATO base.

Chapter 3

1. Later, as the traplines spread further along the main inland river systems, the families spent the winter at one of the developing communities of Mud Lake or North West River while the trapper worked from a main cabin at the beginning of his trapline.

2. As a river, North West River is a term seldom used, but refers to the part of the river system which collects the three rivers and feeds them into Lake Melville.

Chapter 4

1. Social characters evolve out of, and are therefore based on, the actual experiences of North West River Settlers. Since the following discussion requires that both experiences *and* social characters be considered side by side, quotation marks are used to distinguish social characters from actual experiences.

2. William Mesher possibly came out to Labrador with the DeQuetteville Company from Jersey. The company had a base in Blanc Sablon.

3. Documents for the Labrador Boundary Dispute, which took place between Newfoundland and Quebec in 1927, when the present Provincial boundary was settled upon, were collected by Sir Patrick T. McGrath, and are kept in the Provincial Archives in St. John's.

4. William Blake senior is listed in the Slade's Company ledger for the years 1792–98 and again in 1802–09. William Blake junior first appears in the ledgers in 1794. The ledgers record goods traded out to men

over-wintering along the southern Labrador shore. It is possible that William Blake had moved into Hamilton Inlet to over-winter.

5. George Blake is mentioned as a 'planter' in the Hudson's Bay Company journal for 1845.

6. The Baikie family were originally 'Odal' landowners of Norse descent and once owned Tankerton House which now houses Orkney Museum. However, it is unlikely that the branch of the family from which Thomas Baikie came were wealthy since he came out to Labrador in search of work with the Hudson's Bay Company during a relatively prosperous period in Orkney history.

7. That Newfoundlanders form an ambiguous group in the community, and are able to espouse both 'newcomer' and 'oldtimer' social characters in different situations, is also illustrated by several other examples from my fieldnotes. Members of the women's darts team for which I played often broke into alcohol-induced tirades against Newfoundlanders which were nevertheless interjected with comments affirming the place of Newfoundlanders in the community. Conversations between community members would suddenly become heated when the role of the Newfoundland Provincial Government in Labrador affairs was discussed. I was also told on a number of occasions in response to a question about the low rate of marriages between Settlers and Indians, that only Newfoundlanders would be silly enough to marry Indians. Despite such displays of 'otherness' on the part of community members, Newfoundlanders have been marrying into the community for generations, and many North West River inhabitants can claim (and sometimes boast of) part Newfoundlander ancestry.

8. The phenomenon is described in various studies of the north. Both Riches and Koster, in Paine (1977) describe the groups of white Euro-Canadian outsiders that form in the arctic, and the outsider group in North West River is essentially the same.

Chapter 5

1. All names used henceforth are pseudonyms.

2. I am not using this term in the strictest sense intended by van Gennep (1966) since there are no specific ceremonies associated with the trapper's first trip inland, other than the celebrations which usually marked the beginning of the autumn journey inland, (departure was accompanied by the firing of guns), and Christmas return (when there were square-dances in the community), and teasing by seasoned fellow trappers. Women, often sweethearts or sisters, would make small items associated with trapping, such as a 'prog bag' (a small decorated pouch for carrying shot, tobacco, twine etc) or gun case, to give as gifts, although this was not necessarily for the trapper's first trip.

3. A lake north of the community, but the name is also used here to refer to the hunting and trapping country around the lake.

4. A tilt is barely big enough to stand up in, has no windows and only a

very low, narrow entrance. It is used as a shelter, strategically placed at a day's walking distance from the last tilt along a trapline, in which the trapper would spend the night. Larger shelters, called cabins, are also situated along traplines — usually at the beginning, where furs and stores are kept.

5. Traplines can be almost any length allowed for by the terrain. They usually follow the wooded valleys of small rivers and lakes, often starting inland from a point along a main riverbank, where a cabin or tilt is situated. The route, or 'path,' taken inland cuts through a variety of terrains in order that a selection of animals can be caught. There is at least a distance of ten miles between traplines based along the same riverbank, and traplines seldom intersect each other.

6. The small Settler community of Mud Lake was often the first stopping-place for trappers on their way to traplines along the Hamilton (or Grand) River. Outward-bound trappers took stock of their supplies here, and it signalled the end of the journey for returning trappers, often providing much-needed food and shelter. The Indians passed through the community on their way to the North Shore of Quebec.

Chapter 6

1. There are three variants of Innu Aimun, one of which is spoken by the Indians of Davis Inlet. However, here Alfred is referring to the same group of Indians he recognizes from his trapping days in the Mealy Mountains, and they speak the same variant of Innu Aimun as he remembers from the past.

2. That the Youth Group is run under the auspices of the United Church is not particularly significant in the selection of young people attending the meetings, since the criterion for membership is restricted solely by age, (fourteen to eighteen years). Likewise, the volunteers running the group are not members of the United Church; at the time under discussion they consisted of two Mennonite missionaries, several Katimavik workers and myself.

3. At an earlier meeting, I had suggested the theme of ethnic relations as a possible topic for discussion. The term racism was substituted because nobody in the group had heard of the term 'ethnic relations.'

4. The leader read out her questions one at a time and asked each member to write an immediate reaction to the question on a piece of paper. The group was divided arbitrarily into four smaller groups in order to discuss everyone's responses to the questions. These groups then reconvened and a spokesperson from each group read out the joint responses of their group's discussion of the questions, eliciting a general discussion.

5. There was a trial period in which Indians attended Lake Melville High School, the high school attended by Settler children in North West River. The attempt at amalgamating the two groups for the purpose of schooling failed, and the reason given was that the Indian parents

wanted their children to attend a Catholic school. However, from the comments of a few people who were part of the scheme, both Indians and Settlers, it would seem that the Indian children were never accepted by the Settler children.

6. Lucy's mother is Indian.

7. At the time I was in North West River, Rigolet had the nickname of 'Fraggle Rock' — after a popular comic puppet show which was viewed on television by members of both communities. Similarly, it also had the name Danger Bay!

8. In 1979 I collected maps by Settler and Indian children, drawn during geography classes held in their respective schools, as fieldwork data towards an undergraduate honours dissertation (Plaice 1980). The maps of the Settler children covered the north bank of the town, stopping at the river bank by the cable car shelter. Likewise, the maps drawn by Indian children showed only the south bank of the town, despite the fact that I asked them to draw the town of North West River, which at that time included both Sheshatshit and North West River.

9. It was hoped that the uranium mining would prove to be a viable operation at some future date for Brinco, or another such mineral exploration company.

Chapter 7

1. The conspicuous group — marked by its minority or subordinate position in a society. Because Upalongers form only a small section of the population, they are a more noticeable group than Downalongers, and Downalong values and perceptions are more widespread.

2. This has begun to change; an Upalonger formed part of the 1987–88 Town Council, and a small business has recently been established in Upalong.

3. Zimmerly (1975:237–238) describes a similar phenomenon in his discussion of the impact of wage-labour on the trapping economy brought about by the construction of Goose Bay Airbase. He quotes Findlay from an article in *Maclean's* magazine for June 1943: "Employment of Montagnais/Naskapi Indians was almost nil. The contractors tried to hire them to work without much success. They would work a couple of days and then drift away.'"

Chapter 8

1. Some Settlers feel that the term 'Settler' dispossesses them from Labrador, since a Settler cannot be considered to be indigenous. This is in contrast to the term 'Labradorian,' and the sense of territorial belonging which it promotes.

2. Most Inuit live in neighbouring communities at some distance from North West River. Of the Inuit families living in North West River, two form mixed marriages between Settlers and Inuit. They are from the

neighbouring community of Rigolet, and they migrate between their home community and North West River. However, one Inuit family remains from the 1959 resettlement of the northern communities (when four families were moved to North West River from Nutak.) This family speaks no English and is isolated from mainstream North West River society. Most Inuit have settled on the coast, and therefore are not so noticeable as a culture to North West River Settlers.

References

Anderson, A. B. and J. S. Frideres 1981 *Ethnicity in Canada: Theoretical Perspectives*. Toronto: Butterworths.

Baikie, Margaret 1976 "Happy Valley Goose Bay." *Them Days Publications*.

Bailey, Patrick 1971 *The Island Series: Orkney*. Newton Abbott, David and Charles.

Barth, Fredrik 1969 *Ethnic Groups and Boundaries: The Social Organisation of Cultural Difference*. Boston: Little, Brown and Company.

Ben-Dor, Shmuel 1961 *Makkovik: Eskimos and Settlers in a Labrador Community*. St. John's: Institute of Social and Economic Research, Memorial University of Newfoundland.

Berghe, Pierre Van den 1973 "Pluralism." In J. J. Honigmann (ed.), *Handbook of Social and Cultural Anthropology*. Chicago: Rand McNally.

Bonacich, Edna 1972 "A Theory of Ethnic Antagonism: The Split Labour Market." *American Sociological Review*, 37:547–59.

Brantenburg, Terje 1977 "Ethnic Values and Ethnic Recruitment." In Robert Paine (ed.), *The White Arctic*. St. John's: Institute of Social and Economic Research, Memorial University of Newfoundland.

Braroe, Neils Winther 1975 *Indian and White: Self-Image and Interaction in a Canadian Plains Community*. Stanford: Stanford University Press.

Brice-Bennett, Carol (ed.) 1977 *Our Footprints are Everywhere*. Nain: Labrador Press.

Brown, Andrew and Ralph Gray 1951 "Labrador Canoe Adventure." *The National Geographic Magazine*, C(1):65–99.

Campbell, Lydia 1980 *Sketches of Labrador Life*. Happy Valley-Goose Bay: *Them Days Publications* (reproduced from *The Evening Herald*, December 3–7, 10, 12–13, 18, 20, 24 1894, and February 6 1895).

Carstens, Peter 1971 "Coercion and Change." In R. J. Ossenberg (ed.), *Canadian Society: Pluralism, Change and Conflict*. Scarborough: Prentice Hall.

Cardinal, Harold 1969 *The Unjust Society*. Edmonton: Hurtig.

_____ 1977 *The Rebirth of Canada's Indians*. Edmonton: Hurtig.

Cartwright, George 1792 *A Journal of Transactions and Events During Residence of Nearly Sixteen Years on Labrador*, vols I–III. London: Newark.

Clouston, J. Storer 1937 "Orkney and the Hudson's Bay Company." *The Beaver*, December pp. 4–8 and September pp. 37–39.

Cohen, Abner (ed.) 1974 *Urban Ethnicity*. London: Tavistock.

Cooke, Alan 1979 "L'independence des Naskapis et le Caribou." *Recherches Amerindiennes au Quebec*, IX(1–2):99–104. (Reprinted in English by the Centre for Northern Studies, McGill University, Montreal, Quebec.)

Damas, David (ed.) 1969 *Contributions To Anthropology: Band Societies*. Proceedings of the Conference on Band Organisation. Ottawa: Queen's Printers for Canada.

Davies, W. H. A. 1843 "Notes on Esquimaux Bay and the Surrounding Country." *Transactions*, 4(1):70–94. Literary and Historical Society of Quebec.

Dyck, Noel (ed.) 1985 *Indigenous Peoples and the Nation-State. Fourth World Politics in Canada, Australia and Norway*. St. John's: Institute of Social and Economic Research, Memorial University of Newfoundland.

De Vos, George 1975 "Introduction." In George De Vos and Lola Romanucci-Ross (eds.), *Ethnic Identity: Cultural Continuities and Change*. Palo Alto, California: Mayfield Publishing.

_____ and Lola Romanucci-Ross (eds.) 1975 *Ethnic Identity: Cultural Continuities and Change*. Palo Alto, California: Mayfield Publishing.

Eidheim, Harald 1971 *Aspects of the Lappish Minority Situation*. Oslo: Universitetsforlaget.

Elsner, Brother 1857 *Brother Elsner's Report of a Journey from Hopedale to North West River, Esquimaux Bay, in April 1857. London: Periodical Accounts* to the Missions of the Church of the United Brethren, Established among the Hethen.

Epstein, A. L. 1978 *Ethos and Identity: Three Studies in Ethnicity*. London: Tavistock Publications.

Fitzhugh, William 1972 *Environmental Archeology and Cultural Systems in Hamilton Inlet, Labrador*. Smithsonian Contributions to Anthropology, 16. Washington: Smithsonian Institution Press.

Gennep, Arnold van 1966 *The Rites of Passage*. Chicago: Phoenix Books, University of Chicago Press.

Garfinkel, Harold 1952 "The Perception of the Other: A Study in Social Order." Cambridge, Mass.: Harvard University, unpublished Ph.D. thesis.

Glick, Clarence 1955 "Social Roles and Types in Race Relations." In Andrew Lind (ed.), *Race Relations in World Perspective*. Honolulu: University of Hawaii Press.

Gluckman, Max 1965 *Politics, Law and Ritual in Tribal Society*. Chicago: Aldine Publishing Company.

Goffman, Erving 1959 *The Presentation of Self in Everyday Life*. New York: Doubleday.

_____ 1974 *Frame Analysis, An Essay on the Organisation of Experience*. Cambridge, Mass.: Harvard University Press.

Goldring, Phillip 1980 *Papers on the Labour System of the Hudson's Bay Company 1821–1900*, vol. 1. Ottawa: Natural History Sites and Parks Branch Manuscript Series, 412.

Gosling, W. G. 1910 *Labrador: Its Discovery, Exploration and Development*. London: Alston Rivers.

Goudie, Elizabeth 1973 *Woman of Labrador*. Toronto: Peter Martin Associates.

Grenfell, Wilfred Thomason 1902 "Labrador Jottings." In *Toilers of the Sea*. Publication of the Royal National Mission to Deep Sea Fishermen.

_____ 1919 *A Labrador Doctor: Autobiography of Wilfred Thomason Grenfell*. Boston and New York: Houghton Mifflin Company.

_____ 1932 *Forty Years for Labrador*. Boston and New York: Houghton Mifflin Company.

Haugeland, John 1985 *Artificial Intelligence: The Very Idea*. Cambridge, Mass.: MIT Press.

Hallock, Charles 1861 "Three Months in Labrador." *Harpers New Monthly Magazine*, 22(81):577–579, 743–765.

Hancock, W. Gordon 1977 "English Migration to Newfoundland." In John J. Mannion (ed.), *The Peopling of Newfoundland: Essays in Historical Geography*. St. John's: Institute of Social and Economic Research, Memorial University of Newfoundland.

Henriksen, Georg 1973 *Hunters in the Barrens: The Naskapi on the Edge of the White Man's World*. St. John's: Institute of Social and Economic Research, Memorial University of Newfoundland.

Hickson, Thomas 1825 in *Wesleyan Methodist Magazine*. Reprinted in Arminius Young, *One Hundred Years of Mission Work in the Wilds of Labrador*. London: Arthur H. Stockwell, Ltd, 1931.

Honigmann, J. J. 1965 "Social Disintegration in Five Northern Canadian Communities." *The Canadian Review of Sociology and Anthropology* 2:199–214.

_____ (ed.) 1973 *Handbook of Social and Cultural Anthropology*. Chicago: Rand McNally.

Hubbard, Mrs. Leonidas 1908 *A Woman's Way Through Unknown Labrador*. New York: The McClure Company.

Inglis, Gordon 1970 "Canadian Indian Reserve Populations: Some Problems of Conceptualisation." *Northwest Anthropological Research Notes*, 5(1).

Judd, Carol M. and Arthur J. Ray (eds.) 1980 *Old Paths and New Directions: Papers of the Third North American Fur Trade Conference*. Toronto: University of Toronto Press.

Kennedy, John Charles 1982 *Holding the Line: Ethnic Boundaries in a Labrador Community*. St. John's: Institute of Economic and Social Research, Memorial University of Newfoundland.

_____ 1985 "Community Development in Labrador: The Grenfell Experiment." Unpublished manuscript, St. John's: Memorial University of Newfoundland.

Kerr, J. Lennox 1959 *Wilfred Grenfell: His Life and Works*. New York: Dodd, Mead and Company.

Keyes, Charles F. (ed.) 1981 *Ethnic Change*. Seattle: University of Washington Press.

Koster, Ditte 1977 "Why is He Here?: White Gossip." In Robert Paine (ed.), *The White Arctic: Anthropological Essays on Tutelage and Ethnicity*. St. John's: Institute of Social and Economic Research, Memorial University of Newfoundland.

Leacock, Eleanor 1954 "Montagnais Hunting Territory and the Fur Trade." *American Anthropologist,*. Memoir No. 78, 56(5) part two. Washington: Smithsonian Institute Press.

_____ 1955 "Matrilocality in a Simple Hunting Economy (Montagnais-Naskapi)." *South Western Journal of Anthropology* II.

_____ 1969 "The Montagnais-Naskapi Band." In David Damas (ed.), *Contributions To Anthropology: Band Societies*. Proceedings of the Conference on Band Organisation Ottawa: Queen's Printers for Canada.

Levi-Strauss, Claude 1966 *The Savage Mind*. Chicago: The University of Chicago Press.

Lind, Andrew W. (ed.) 1955 *Race Relations in World Perspective: Papers Read at the Conference on Race Relations in World Perspective, Honolulu, 1954*. Honolulu: University of Hawaii Press.

Linklater, Eric 1965 *Orkneys and Shetland: An Historical, Geographical, Social and Scenic Survey*. London: Robert Hale.

Lithman, Yngve Georg 1978 *The Community Apart: A Case Study of a Canadian Indian Reserve Community*. Stockholm: University of Stockholm.

Low, Albert Peter 1896 *Report on Explorations in the Labrador Peninsula Along the East Main, Koksoak, Hamilton, Manicuagan and Portions of other Rivers in 1892-93-94-95*. Geological Survey of Canada, Annual Report (New Series), 8(L).

Manuel, George and Michael Posluns 1974 *The Fourth World: An Indian Reality*. Toronto: MacMillan Company of Canada.

Mailhot, Jose 1986a "Beyond Everyone's Horizon Stand the Naskapi." *Ethnohistory* 33(4):384–418.

_____ 1986b "Territorial Mobility among the Montagnais-Naskapi of Labrador." *Anthropologica*. New Series, 18(1–2):92–107.

_____ 1988 "The Naskapi Syndrome in the Community of Sheshatshit." Seminar given for the Institute of Social and Economic Research January, 1988.

Mann, W. E. (ed.) 1970 *Social and Cultural Change in Canada*. Toronto: Copp Clark.

Mannion, John J. (ed.) 1977 *The Peopling of Newfoundland: Essays in Historical Geography*. St. John's: Institute of Social and Economic Research, Memorial University of Newfoundland.

Marwick, Ernest "Journey From Serfdom." Unpublished manuscript, Kirkwall: Orkney Archives.

Matthews, Keith 1968a "A History of the West of England—Newfoundland Fishery." Unpublished PhD thesis, Oxford: University of Oxford.

------------- 1968b *The West Country Merchants in Newfoundland*. Newfoundland Historical Society Lecture (1–12), St. John's: Newfoundland Historical Society.

McCall, Christopher 1983 "Ethnicity, Class and the State." Unpublished manuscript, Montreal: McGill University.

McGee, John T. 1961 *Cultural Stability and Change Among the Montagnais Indians of the Lake Melville Region of Labrador*. The Catholic University of America, Anthropological Series, no. 19. Washington: The Catholic University of America Press.

McLean, John 1849 *Notes of Twenty Five Year's Service in the Hudson's Bay Territory*. London: Richard Bentley, New Burlington Street, in two volumes (republished by the Hudson's Bay Company).

Merrick, Elliott 1933 *True North*. New York: Charles Scribner's Son.

Mitchell, J. Clyde 1956 *The Kalela Dance*. Rhodes-Livingstone Paper No. 27. Manchester: Manchester University Press.

Moores, Janet 1985 "The Life and Death of the Grenfell Association in North West River, Labrador." Unpublished undergraduate paper, St. John's: Memorial University of Newfoundland.

Murdock, George Peter 1949 *Social Structure*. New York: The Macmillan Company.

_____ 1967 *Ethnographic Atlas*. Pittsburgh: University of Pittsburgh Press.

New Statistical Account of Scotland, The 1845, London: Blackwood and Son.

Nicks, John 1980 "Orkneymen and the HBC 1780–1821." In Carol M. Judd and Arthur J. Ray (eds.), *Old Paths and New Directions: Papers of the Third North American Fur Trade Conference*. Toronto: University of Toronto Press.

Ossenberg, R. J. (ed.) 1971 *Canadian Society: Pluralism, Change and Conflict*. Scarborough: Prentice Hall.

Paddon, Harry L. 1920 "Central Labrador Today." In *Among the Deep Sea Fishers*. Publication of the International Grenfell Association, 17(4).

Paine, Robert 1971 "A Theory of Patronage and Brokerage." In Robert Paine (ed.), *Patrons and Brokers in the East Arctic*. St. John's: Institute of Social and Economic Research, Memorial University of Newfoundland.

_____ (ed.) 1971 *Patrons and Brokers in the East Arctic*. St. John's: Institute of Social and Economic Research, Memorial University of Newfoundland.

_____ (ed.) 1977 *The White Arctic: Anthropological Essays on Tutelage and Ethnicity*. St. John's: Institute of Social and Economic Research, Memorial University of Newfoundland.

_____ (ed.) 1985 *Advocacy and Anthropology: First Encounters*. St. John's: Institute of Social and Economic Research, Memorial University of Newfoundland.

Plaice, Evelyn Mary 1980 "This Land is My Land—Nin Ume Ntassi: Conflict over Land Between Indians and Settlers in Central Labrador." Unpublished honours dissertation, Oxford: Oxford Polytechnic.

Pontings, J. Rick and Roger Gibbins 1976 *Out of Irrelevance*. Toronto: Butterworths.

Porter, John 1965 *The Vertical Mosaic: An Analysis of Social Class and Power in Canada*. Toronto: University of Toronto Press.

Rapport, Nigel 1983 "Fred, Doris and Florence: Of Worldviews in the English Dale of Bant." Series of seminars based on unpublished Doctoral thesis. Mimeograph, St. John's: Institute of Social and Economic Research, Memorial University of Newfoundland.

Riches, David 1977 "Neighbours in the Bush: White Cliques." In Robert Paine (ed.), *The White Arctic: Anthropological Essays on Tutelage and Ethnicity*. St. John's: Institute of Social and Economic Research, Memorial University of Newfoundland.

Schutz, Alfred and Thomas Luckmann 1974 *The Structures of the Life-World*. London: Heinemann.

Schwimmer, Eric 1972 "Symbolic Competition." In *Anthropologica*. New Series, 14(2):117–155.

Shearer, John, W. Groundwater and J.D. Mackay 1967 *The New Orkney Book*. London: Thomas Nelson and Sons.

Shibutani, Tamotsu, and Kian Kwan 1965 *Ethnic Stratification*. New York: Macmillan.

Sinclair, Sir John 1927 *The Orkney Parishes: Containing the Statistical Account of Orkney 1795-1798, Drawn from the Communications of the Different Ministers of the Different Parishes.* Republished with an Introduction by J. Storer Clouston. Kirkwall: W. R. Mackintosh, The Orcadian Office.

Smith, P. 1975 *Brinco: The Story of Churchill Falls.* Toronto: McClelland and Stewart.

Speck, Frank Goldsmith 1935 *Naskapi: The Savage Hunters of the Labrador Peninsula.* Norman: University of Oklahoma Press.

_____ 1942 *Montagnais-Naskapi Bands and Family Hunting Districts of the Central and Southern Labrador Peninsula.* Proceedings of the American Philosophical Society, 85.

Stymeist, David H. 1975 *Ethnics and Indians: Social Relations in a Northwest Ontario Town.* Toronto: Peter Martin Associates.

Tanner, Adrian 1977 "Indian Land Use and Land Tenure in the Southern Half of Labrador." Unpublished report prepared for the NMIA, Sheshatshiu, Labrador. St. John's: Memorial University of Newfoundland.

Tanner, Adrian (ed.) 1983 *The Politics of Indianness. Case Studies of Native Ethnopolitics in Canada.* St. John's: Institute of Social and Economic Research, Memorial University of Newfoundland.

Tanner, Vaino 1944 *Outlines of the Geography, Life and Customs of Newfoundland-Labrador.* Acta Geographica 8(1), two volumes. Helsinki: Oy. Tilgmann Ab.

Teal, Greg and David Bai 1981 "Class Dismissed: A Weberian Critique of Class and Ethnicity." *Culture* 1(1):96–102.

Thompson, E. P. 1978 *The Making of the English Working Class.* London: Penguin.

Thomson, William P. L. 1981 *The Little General and the Rousay Crofters: Crisis and Conflict on an Orkney Crofting Estate.* Edinburgh: J. Donald Publishers.

_____ 1983 *Kelp Making in Orkney.* Kirkwall: The Orkney Press.

Thornton, Patricia 1977 "The Demographic and Mercantile Bases of Initial Permanent Settlement in the Strait of Belle Isle." In John J. Mannion (ed.), *The Peopling of Newfoundland: Essays in Historical Geography.* St. John's: Institute of Social and Economic Research, Memorial University of Newfoundland.

Wallace, Dillon 1915 *The Lure of the Labrador Wild.* Toronto: Hodder and Stoughton.

Wallace, W. S. 1932 *John McLean's Notes of a Twenty-Five Year's Service in the Hudson's Bay Territory.* Toronto: The Champlain Society.

Willson, Beckles 1915 *The Life of Lord Strathcona and Mount Royal.* Cambridge: The Riverside Press (Houghton Mifflin Company).

Young, Arminius 1931 *One Hundred Years of Mission Work in the Wilds of Labrador*. London: Arthur H. Stockwell, Ltd.

Zimmerly, William David 1975 *Cain's Land Revisited: Culture Change in Central Labrador, 1775–1972*. St. John's: Institute of Social and Economic Research, Memorial University of Newfoundland.

Manuscript Sources

Bird, Thomas (English Merchant) 1824–1844 Accounts, letterbooks, ledgers and inventories of Thomas Bird Provincial Archives of Newfoundland and Labrador, reference no. P3/B/18, private papers collection.

McGrath, Sir Patrick T. 1927. Research material compiled by P. T. McGrath, regarding the Labrador Boundary Dispute. Provincial Archives of Newfoundland and Labrador, reference number P.4/17, private papers collection.

Slade and Sons, Fogo (merchants) Ledgers, day books, account books, letter books, correspondence c. 1780–1880. Provincial Archives of Newfoundland and Labrador, reference no. P7/A/6, private papers collection.

ISER BOOKS

Studies

40 **The Native Game: Settler Perceptions of Indian/Settler Relations in Central Labrador**—Evelyn Plaice

39 **The Northern Route: An Ethnography of Refugee Experiences**—Lisa Gilad

38 **Hostage to Fortune: Bantry Bay and the Encounter with Gulf Oil**—Chris Eipper

37 **Language and Poverty: The Persistence of Scottish Gaelic in Eastern Canada**—Gilbert Foster

36 **A Public Nuisance: A History of the Mummers Troupe**—Chris Brookes

35 **Listen While I Tell You: A Story of the Jews of St. John's, Newfoundland**—Alison Kahn

34 **Talking Violence: An Anthropological Interpretation of Conversation in the City**—Nigel Rapport

33 **"To Each His Own": William Coaker and the Fishermen's Protective Union in Newfoundland Politics, 1908–1925**—Ian D.H. McDonald, edited by J.K Hiller

32 **Sea Change: A Shetland Society, 1970–79**—Reginald Byron

31 **From Traps to Draggers: Domestic Commodity Production in Northwest Newfoundland, 1850–1982**—Peter Sinclair

30 **The Challenge of Oil: Newfoundland's Quest for Controlled Development**—J.D. House

29 **Sons and Seals: A Voyage to the Ice**—Guy Wright

28 **Blood and Nerves: An Ethnographic Focus on Menopause**—Dona Lee Davis

27 **Holding the Line: Ethnic Boundaries in a Northern Labrador Community**—John Kennedy

26 **'Power Begins at the Cod End': The Newfoundland Trawlermen's Strike, 1974–75**—David Macdonald

25 **Terranova: The Ethos and Luck of Deep-Sea Fishermen**—Joseba Zulaika (in Canada only)

24 **"Bloody Decks and a Bumper Crop": The Rhetoric of Sealing Counter-Protest**—Cynthia Lamson

23 **Bringing Home Animals: Religious Ideology and Mode of Production of the Mistassini Cree Hunters**—Adrian Tanner (in Canada only)

22 **Bureaucracy and World View: Studies in the Logic of Official Interpretation** — Don Handelman and Elliott Leyton

21 **If You Don't Be Good: Verbal Social Control in Newfoundland** — John Widdowson

20 **You Never Know What They Might Do: Mental Illness in Outport Newfoundland** — Paul S. Dinham

19 **The Decay of Trade: An Economic History of the Newfoundland Saltfish Trade, 1935–1965** — David Alexander

18 **Manpower and Educational Development in Newfoundland** — S.S. Mensinkai and M.Q. Dalvi

17 **Ancient People of Port au Choix: The Excavation of an Archaic Indian Cemetery in Newfoundland** — James A. Tuck

16 **Cain's Land Revisited: Culture Change in Central Labrador, 1775–1972** — David Zimmerly

15 **The One Blood: Kinship and Class in an Irish Village** — Elliott Leyton

14 **The Management of Myths: The Politics of Legitimation in a Newfoundland Community** — A.P. Cohen (in North America only)

13 **Beluga Hunters: An Archaeological Reconstruction of the History and Culture of the Mackenzie Delta Kittegaryumiut** — Robert McGhee

12 **Hunters in the Barrens: The Naskapi on the Edge of the White Man's World** — Georg Henriksen

11 **Now, Whose Fault is That? The Struggle for Self-Esteem in the Face of Chronic Unemployment** — Cato Wadel

10 **Craftsman-Client Contracts: Interpersonal Relations in a Newfoundland Fishing Community** — Louis Chiaramonte

9 **Newfoundland Fishermen in the Age of Industry: A Sociology of Economic Dualism** — Ottar Brox

8 **Public Policy and Community Protest: The Fogo Case** — Robert L. DeWitt

7 **Marginal Adaptations and Modernization in Newfoundland: A Study of Strategies and Implications of Resettlement and Redevelopment of Outport Fishing Communities** — Cato Wadel

6 **Communities in Decline: An Examination of Household Resettlement in Newfoundland** — N. Iverson and D. Ralph Matthews

5 **Brothers and Rivals: Patrilocality in Savage Cove** — Melvin Firestone

4 **Makkovik: Eskimos and Settlers in a Labrador Community** — Shmuel Ben-Dor

3 **Cat Harbour: A Newfoundland Fishing Settlement** — James C. Faris

2 **Private Cultures and Public Imagery: Interpersonal Relations in a Newfoundland Peasant Society** — John F. Szwed

1 **Fisherman, Logger, Merchant, Miner: Social Change and Industrialism in Three Newfoundland Communities** — Tom Philbrook

Papers

18 **To Work and to Weep: Women in Fishing Economies**—Jane Nadel-Klein and Dona Lee Davis (eds.)

17 **A Question of Survival: The Fisheries and Newfoundland Society**—Peter R. Sinclair (ed.)

16 **Fish Versus Oil: Resources and Rural Development in North Atlantic Societies**—J.D. House (ed.)

15 **Advocacy and Anthropology: First Encounters**—Robert Paine (ed.)

14 **Indigenous Peoples and the Nation-State: Fourth World Politics in Canada, Australia and Norway**—Noel Dyck (ed.)

13 **Minorities and Mother Country Imagery**—Gerald Gold (ed.)

12 **The Politics of Indianness: Case Studies of Native Ethnopolitics in Canada**—Adrian Tanner (ed.)

11 **Belonging: Identity and Social Organisation in British Rural Cultures**—Anthony P. Cohen (ed.) (in North America only)

10 **Politically Speaking: Cross-Cultural Studies of Rhetoric**—Robert Paine (ed.)

 9 **A House Divided? Anthropological Studies of Factionalism**—M. Silverman and R.F. Salisbury (eds.)

 8 **The Peopling of Newfoundland: Essays in Historical Geography**—John J. Mannion (ed.)

 7 **The White Arctic: Anthropological Essays on Tutelage and Ethnicity**—Robert Paine (ed.)

 6 **Consequences of Offshore Oil and Gas—Norway, Scotland and Newfoundland**—M.J. Scarlett (ed.)

 5 **North Atlantic Fishermen: Anthropological Essays on Modern Fishing**—Raoul Andersen and Cato Wadel (eds.)

 4 **Intermediate Adaptation in Newfoundland and the Arctic: A Strategy of Social and Economic Development**—Milton M.R. Freeman (ed.)

 3 **The Compact: Selected Dimensions of Friendship**—Elliott Leyton (ed.)

 2 **Patrons and Brokers in the East Arctic**—Robert Paine (ed.)

 1 **Viewpoints on Communities in Crisis**—Michael L. Skolnik (ed.)

Mailing Address:
    ISER Books (Institute of Social and Economic Research)
    Memorial University of Newfoundland
    St. John's, Newfoundland, Canada, A1C 5S7

Printed in Canada